How I Got This Way

ALSO BY PATRICK F. McMANUS

Kid Camping from Aaaaiii! to Zip
A Fine and Pleasant Misery
They Shoot Canoes, Don't They?
Never Sniff a Gift Fish
The Grasshopper Trap
Rubber Legs and White Tail-Hairs
The Night the Bear Ate Goombaw
Whatchagot Stew
(with Patricia "The Troll" McManus Gass)
Real Ponies Don't Go Oink!
The Good Samaritan Strikes Again

Patrick F. McManus

How
I Got
This Way

Henry Holt and Company   New York

Henry Holt and Company, Inc.
Publishers since 1866
115 West 18th Street
New York, New York 10011

Henry Holt® is a registered trademark
of Henry Holt and Company, Inc.

Published in Canada by Fitzhenry & Whiteside Ltd.,
195 Allstate Parkway, Markham, Ontario L3R 4T8.

Library of Congress Cataloging-in-Publication Data
McManus, Patrick F.
How I got this way / Patrick F. McManus. — 1st ed.
p.   cm.
1. American wit and humor.   I. Title.
PN6162.M34894   1994   94-16971
814'.54—dc20   CIP

ISBN 0-8050-3481-1

Henry Holt books are available for special promotions
and premiums. For details contact: Director, Special Markets.

First Edition—1994

Designed by Betty Lew

Printed in the United States of America
All first editions are printed on acid-free paper. ∞

10 9 8 7 6 5 4 3 2 1

Contents

How I Got This Way

How I Got This Way, Part I

A FEW YEARS ago, my friend Dave Lisaius and I were in my pickup camper, waiting out a storm high up in the Idaho Rockies. Dave sprawled on the cab-over bed while I prepared lunch. The conversation turned to hospitals, possibly because I was preparing lunch, and I remarked that I hadn't been hospitalized since I was five years old.

"How come you were in the hospital then?" Dave asked, careful to conceal behind a yawn his fascination with this intriguing bit of McManus lore.

"Oh, I fell out of a moving bus and landed on my head," I explained.

Dave laughed so hard he almost fell off the bed and landed on *his* head. Eventually, his paroxysm of mirth subsided to a few spasmodic shrieks and howls.

"I didn't think breaking my head was that funny," I said, still puzzled by Dave's unseemly outburst.

"Oh, it isn't!" he choked out, mopping up tears with his shirtsleeve. "But it explains *so much!*"

Dave at the time was a bank president but otherwise fairly decent, often enjoying extended periods of lucidity. Had I evoked this mirthful reaction only from Dave, I would have thought nothing of it. He is not exactly the epitome of normality himself. The problem was, I had provoked similar responses from other individuals on countless occasions. Melba Peachbottom, the prettiest girl in our high school, had almost burst a gut when I casually asked her out on a date. "You're so funny!" she cried. When I turned out for baseball, the coach laughed himself sick. "Stop! Please! No more jokes, McManus!" Sometimes in a restaurant I will glance up and notice a pretty woman across the room smiling at me in obvious bemusement. All I'm doing is drinking a glass of water. Suavely. I smile back and dribble water down my tie. The woman laughs and returns to her salad. I've never been much good at flirtation.

Just this morning I rushed onto a plane at the Minneapolis airport. My boarding pass indicated my seat was 17F. The rows of seats stopped at 16. It's fortunate that they did. Otherwise, I would have ended up in Baltimore instead of Spokane, my intended destination. No doubt a flight attendant would have announced that the plane was headed for Baltimore, but I never listen to those announcements. They get on my nerves. It's possible that the flight attendants would have noticed they had one more passenger for Baltimore than they were supposed to have, but that assumes some guy bound for Baltimore didn't absentmindedly get on the plane for Spokane—such a coincidence is commonplace in my life. Therefore each plane would have had the proper number of passengers, and I would have ended up walking around an airport parking garage in Baltimore looking for my car and eventually reporting it as stolen. "We've located your car, sir," the police would say. "The thieves left it at an airport garage in Spokane."

I have a lot of trouble finding my car. A few weeks ago, I came out of our local library and checked every space in the parking lot, my standard ritual, and my car wasn't in any of them. Just as I was about to report it as stolen, I remembered that I had walked to the library, not driven. My wife, Bun, doesn't like me to go out alone anymore.

Once, I returned home from work, hung up my coat, dropped my briefcase on the floor, and walked into the kitchen. Bun was at the stove cooking supper. She seemed different. "You're home early," she said, without looking up. She sounded different, too. Oddly, she appeared much taller than she had that morning. Then she turned around. There was a strange woman in my house cooking supper! We went through the usual leaping and yelling and feinting at each other that occurs on such occasions, until at last recognition dawned, she being the wife and mother of the family to whom I had sold our house the previous month. It was an exhilarating and memorable experience for both of us, and I know it considerably enriched the lady's conversational repertoire of humorous anecdotes, because I heard the story repeated around town for some years afterwards. It's that sort of thing that can easily give rise to a mistaken impression in a person's community that he possesses certain peculiarities. No one seemed to believe that the fault lay with my car, which, forgetting we had moved, returned to the same old garage it had been using for the previous five years and deposited me at a house that was no longer mine. Stupid car!

During a hunting trip in the wintry mountains of Idaho,

I injured my leg in a fall through a tangle of fallen trees. It soon became apparent that I wouldn't be able to make it to the rendezvous with my hunting companions, so I did the only sensible thing. I built a lean-to and a fire and prepared to spend the night out. Every year people die in the woods, because they don't have enough sense to follow this practice. I was perfectly safe and comfortable and enjoying the experience, except for the occasional sounds of Sasquatches passing by. About two o'clock in the morning, I was found by a search-and-rescue team out of Bonners Ferry, Idaho. Local weekly newspaper headline: LOST PAT MCMANUS SAVED BY SEARCHERS, FAKES LEG INJURY. That headline could just as easily have read, SERIOUSLY INJURED PAT MCMANUS, USING EXPERT WOODSMAN SKILLS, SAVES OWN LIFE AGAINST IMPOSSIBLE ODDS. But no, the headline writer had to contribute to the legend of Pat McManus as inept person, lost person, absentminded person. Once one becomes a legend, it is impossible to outlive it. I have always wanted to become a legend, but this isn't the one.

People are always rushing to my aid when I'm not in trouble. They seem to relish rescuing me. If you were to believe the stories, I have been rescued by approximately 5,000 people. Once I was standing at a candy vending machine with nothing more on my mind than trying to choose between a Milky Way and a Snickers. A woman I scarcely knew came up to me and put a hand on my shoulder. "I don't know what's troubling you," she said, "but it can't be that bad, dear. Sometimes problems can just seem overwhelming. Let's go have a cup of coffee and talk about it." What could I do, tell her my only problem was choosing between a Milky Way and a Snickers? I went and had coffee with her and made up a cock-and-bull story about an identity crisis or some such thing. After we had talked, she said, "Don't you feel better now?" I said yes, and I did, too, because I had made up my mind. I'd go for the Snickers.

What got me to thinking about all this was Dave Lisaius's comment about my falling on my head at age five: "It explains so much!" I decided the time had come to reveal how I got this way.

Falling on my head had nothing to do with it, but here's what happened anyway. My family and I were transferring between trains on different sides of a city. The railroad bus that transported us had a door at each row of seats, for what reason I don't know, unless for instant evacuation of all passengers in case of a calamity. As the bus sped on its way, I began exploring the mechanism of the door handle. Through no fault of my own—even our lawyers said so—the door popped open and shot me into empty space. To this day I can remember the exhilaration of that first flight, even though it lasted but a second. I didn't land on my head right away, choosing to put that off until the second or third bounce, an early indication of my inherent good sense. By the time I stopped bouncing, I had pretty well concluded that tinkering with the door mechanism hadn't been such a good idea, as various parts of my anatomy seemed to have undergone major rearrangement. The worst was yet to come, however.

Although the visits to doctors and clinics and hospitals continued for several years, the worst part was my imprisonment in a hospital. Within a couple of days, I was up and around, much to the consternation of the nurses, who were of the opinion that some of my essential parts might fall off. The nurses raised a big fuss, apparently for the purpose of impressing upon me that I was supposed to stay in bed instead of fiddling with the mechanism that opened the window above a parking lot five stories down. After being subjected to a frightening display of hysteria by the nurses, I decided it was better to stay in bed, rather than put up with their ranting and raving and screeching. My only entertainment was a little man who marched around inside my head beating a drum, and that quickly palled. Endless waves of boredom washed over me for hours, days, and weeks, with no land in sight. I began to make up little stories, often about nurses being eaten by monsters, one of my favorite plots. The nurses must have liked me, though, because when the day finally came for me to leave the hospital, a group of them gathered around laughing and smiling and applauding my departure. Several even leaped in the air and clicked their heels, which I thought a bit excessive but appreciated anyway.

My father died when I was six years old, leaving my mother as the sole support of our family, which then consisted of Mom, my grandmother, my sister, Patricia "The Troll," and me, now the lone male in a family of women. Mom earned our livelihood by teaching school, an occupation that at the time absolutely forbid its practitioners to smoke, drink, or gamble, none of which my mother did to excess. Well, at least she never drank to excess or even much at all. Two out of three ain't bad.

In addition to her teaching, Mom also farmed. She pretty much single-handedly built a large farmhouse, then cleared the land, and raised wheat and chickens. I think that may have been why she gambled and smoked so much, to take her mind off farming. All by itself, you would think farming might have satisfied her appetite for gambling. It didn't. Then there was her other hobby: smoking. Besides helping to relieve stress, cigarettes at the time were considered particularly good for the heart and lungs. And they were. Without sucking in great deep draughts of smoke and tar and nicotine, most folks wouldn't have got any aerobic benefits at all. A good coughing fit served as a workout. Dedicated smokers could work up a good sweat just from coughing. When they got done with a coughing fit, they relaxed with a cigarette. Smokers didn't worry about getting killed by cigarettes in those days, mostly because they figured something else would get them first. Usually it did. As Mom used to say, something's always stalking you.

I doubt most of the people in our little logging community thought much about death or were even terribly concerned about it. Dying was fairly common among members of our family, and our friends and neighbors did a fair amount of it, too. I don't mean to imply that dying ranked high on anyone's list of favorite activities. But when Death knocked, the person went along with it as best he could, and tried not to raise too much fuss. Death didn't have quite the bad reputation it does now, probably because people were more familiar with it, as if it were some eccentric character in the neighborhood who made a pest of himself: "Oh, for gosh sakes, weird old Mort is knocking on the door again. I wonder who he wants this time?"

I should point out, by the way, that I'm not writing about death merely for the purpose of depressing the reader, nor to get one to stop smoking, cut down on cholesterol, wear a seat belt, take out a membership in a health club, avoid late-night walks through the park, nor jog five miles before work every morning. It seems that if you even mention the word "death" today, your listeners immediately burst into a frenzy of healthful activity. No, my only purpose here is to set in perspective a way of life in a distant time and place that may seem to the modern reader to be crude and harsh and uncivilized, but which in truth was a way of life that was, well, crude and harsh and uncivilized. It explains to some degree how I got this way.

Our lives in those years alternated between famine and famine with an occasional feast as a surprise. Mom taught mostly in little one-room schools scattered throughout the mountains of Idaho. The Great Depression was still under way, and a great many people had retreated into the mountains for its duration. They built little cabins, cut their own firewood, grew big gardens, and harvested fish and game from the streams and forests. They got their light from kerosene lanterns, their water from the creek, and their entertainment from wherever they could find it. It was not a bad life and required very little money, which was a good thing, because that's what most people had.

Mom got a job teaching in a little log-cabin school in a remote mountain valley near Priest Lake in the Panhandle of Idaho. It was there that I entered first grade. I learned to read in approximately one day, and from then on took an extended vacation from the tedium of school. While the other kids were hunched over their books, my mother cracking the whip of learning over their heads, I would wander outside, roam the woods, try to catch trout from the creek, and enjoyed a great sense of freedom. It was a nice way to spend first grade. Mom didn't seem to mind. During the long winters, I exhausted most of the books in the school, not one of which was particularly interesting but better than nothing. Mom spiced up each day by reading for fifteen minutes from books by Mark Twain, Jack London, Herman Melville, Charles Dickens, and other of her favorite authors, thereby giving me a taste for actual literature. During my second grade at this same school, I again roamed far and wide while school was in session, returning to it only when I felt the risk of being subjected to education had sufficiently diminished for the day. Once again, Mom showed no disapproval of my freewheeling ways, and it began to appear that she and I shared the same theories regarding the proper schooling for a young boy. The next year, however, Mom got a job teaching in town, where I assumed I would attend third grade. "Nope," Mom told me. "Second grade." I was astonished and enraged. My own mother had flunked me! The reason for this act of maternal treason, as she wrote on my report card, was "Too many absences." Since we had lived right in the schoolroom, I eventually regarded my flunking second grade on the grounds of too many absences as being a major achievement, and I still do. Much later, as an adult, I realized that my mother had given me a great gift in allowing me to wander in joy and wild abandonment during my first two years of school, and that gift was a sense of freedom. From then on my life was set on a course of someday achieving that same actual freedom once again. I haven't succeeded, but I'm still trying.

The following year we returned to live full time at our farm, where my mother attempted to achieve total self-reliance. She had no faith in the beneficence of government and would have grimly starved us all before accepting charity in any form. I for my part would gladly have voted for charity, but our family didn't operate under a democratic form of government. Mom despised weakness, not of body but of will. She was not particularly fond of order, either, but thrived on chaos, confusion, and crisis, all of which are bountiful in the lives of people who attempt to achieve total self-reliance. Take chickens for instance.

Every year Mom and Gram and Troll took dozens of

chicken lives there on the farm, committed these tiny murders and never even thought twice about it. Probably never even thought once about it. I myself was much too sensitive to participate in the callous slaughter of chickens and rabbits and the occasional hog or steer. In fact, when I was six, I was ridiculed at length by the women for crying over the death of a flower, a trillium I had found growing in the woods. The real reason for my tears, however, I never revealed to anyone. I figured it was better to stick with the trillium and not stretch my luck.

The winter of 1939, the year of first grade, was a particularly hard one, even for North Idaho, and we had been snowbound at the log-cabin school in the mountains for at least half a century, probably longer. Then, suddenly, in early April, chinook winds came up and almost overnight wiped out the snow. Soon bright green blades of grass shot up in the pools of sunshine scattered through the woods, pussy willows budded out along the banks of overflowing creeks, and robins drifted in to check out the new worm crop. Finding ourselves free from winter at last, my mother cranked up our cantankerous old Chevy sedan, and we set off for a wild spree in town. Ten miles or so down the road, the car stopped, possibly because the radiator boiled over or one of the tires had gone flat. I can't remember the exact cause, because I paid little attention to calamities not of my own making. We piled out. I saw right away that this was a problem Mom could solve, whatever it was. She shook a Camel cigarette out of her pack, tapped it on the back of her hand, lit up, and blew a cloud of smoke up into the blue spring sky. Seeing her smoke a cigarette during a predicament always had a calming effect on me. I knew whatever was wrong, she and her cigarette could fix it. Thusly comforted, I wandered off into the boggy woods to explore, and there I came upon the little white trillium. I gouged it up, bulb and all, and carried it back to the car.

"Look, Mom!" I yelled. "I found a flower for you."

Mom glanced up from repairing the car, took a drag on her cigarette, wiped some grease off her face, and, squinting hard through the stream of exhaled smoke, said, "Thanks." She was not one of those gushy mothers who go overboard in expressing gratitude for small cheap gifts clutched in grubby little paws.

On our way back from town, a terrible thing happened. A blizzard blew in. I was sitting in the backseat of the car with the trillium resting on my lap. Our car was a very basic model, and I'm not sure it even had a heater, but if so, it was not one that had worked in my lifetime. Pretty soon we had about as much blizzard inside the car as there was outside. The family started to succumb to frost, as did the trillium. The flower gasped, gave a couple of shudders, wilted over, and died in my lap. As I stared down at it, a great sadness engulfed me.

"My trillium died!" I yelled at my mother. And that's when I began to cry. Mom squinted out through a quarter-size hole she had scraped in the frost on the windshield. The car alternately bucked through snowdrifts and cut figure eights on the icy road.

"Let me get this straight," Mom growled, the tip of the cigarette clamped between her lips glowing brighter in the dark. "You're crying over a stupid flower?" That was when the womenfolk burst into gales of laughter, forgetting for the moment that we might all be found frozen solid in a snowdrift on a remote road in the mountains some weeks hence. I stopped crying, pleased to have introduced a bit of levity into an otherwise tense situation. It occurred to me I might have a talent for humor.

There was something about this incident I never explained to my family, and which has remained a secret all these many years of my having to listen to the story being told about that trillium: I wasn't crying over the death of a flower, but over the death of *spring*. Anyone with an iota of sensibility could have perceived that.

I recount this miserable anecdote only for the purpose of establishing my own keen sensitivity. Otherwise, I wish to hear nothing more of it.

The women in my family, by contrast, possessed approximately the same emotional makeup as a sack of nails. My grandmother, Gram, a short, stout pioneer woman, had spent most of her life cooking in logging camps, where breakfast consisted of five gallons of coffee, fifty steaks, five dozen eggs, ten pounds of bacon, a hundred pancakes, a flatcar of fried potatoes, and a truckload of toast. She got up at three in the morning to prepare breakfast and went to bed after washing the supper dishes. Both her arms would be blistered to the elbows from the wood-fired cookstoves and the huge hot pans and kettles and splattering grease and scalding water. After Gram came to live with us, I'd run in the house yelling, "Ow! Ow! I'm hurt! I'm hurt! Ow! Ow!" Gram would leap up in a panic, crossing herself and murmuring a brief prayer. She assumed anyone making that much of a ruckus must have broken at least two legs and an arm and be bleeding to death for good measure.

"Look, Gram!" I'd yell at her. "I skinned my knee! Ow! Ow!"

"You scared me half to death over a skinned knee?" she would snarl. "Why you big calf!" After a while, I realized

there wasn't much point in expecting a lot of sympathy from
an old woman who had spent so much of her life cooking in
logging camps.

It was almost unheard of for anyone in our family to go
to a hospital or even a doctor. My mother's view seemed to be
that either you got better or you didn't. Once, Troll got a
thorn stuck in her hand, which swelled up into the general
shape and size of a catcher's mitt. The swelling soon went up
her arm, turning it a nice shade of blue-green, one of my
favorite colors at the time. Troll's arm became so ghastly I
would usher my little friends into her room so they could look
at it and see if it made them sick to their stomachs, as I had
predicted.

"There's the arm."

"Yeeesh!"

Still Mom refused to take Troll to the doctor. Even at
that young age, I could see that the Troll's condition might
be terminal, and so I tried to be as nice to her as I could,
being careful to shield her from the fact that bit by bit I was
moving my belongings into her room. One tries to be considerate. Mom eventually hauled the Troll off to the doctor, who
said she only had a bad case of blood poisoning, and, for a
couple of bucks and a modicum of pain, he cured her arm.
Typically, Troll had been fussing about nothing.

Troll, six years older than I, was a powerful creature,
fond of picking me up and bouncing me against a wall or a
tree, apparently as a form of entertainment or, in later years,
merely from force of habit. I was defenseless against her
onslaughts, which could occur at any time of day or night.
She knew magic, too, basic troll magic. She could create illu-
sions out of nothing more than thin air and a shadow or two.
Once, as the two of us were tramping home in winter along a

narrow wooded trail, she stopped and pointed into the shadows. "Shhhh," she said.

"What is it?" I whispered, peering intently into the shadows, knowing from experience it wouldn't be anything good.

"Wolves. Don't you see them?"

"N-no!"

"Are you blind or what?" she hissed. "Can't you see that big shaggy one with the spit dribbling off his jaws?"

"Cripes!"

Not only could I see the wolf, I saw it in perfect detail, a big ol' red tongue lolling out from between sharp white teeth, the frosty fur bristling on the back of his neck, the mean, fiery eyes.

"And here he comes!" the Troll screeched.

My feet spun down through the ice on the trail, found traction in the dirt beneath, and sent me on a flat screaming trajectory toward home, the wolf snapping at my heels all the way. Bursting into the house, I told Mom about the wolves, that they must have got Troll. She said, "Well, in that case, set the table for only three tonight." Troll strolled in a half hour later, claiming to know nothing of wolves. It's a terrible thing for a boy to have a sister six years older than he, and one that does troll magic besides. To this day, many of my lesser organs believe in ghosts, even if my mind doesn't, apparently as a result of Troll having shown me so many apparitions during my formative years.

"See that old man? He's not real."

"He isn't?"

"No, he's a ghost."

"How do you know?"

" 'Cause you can see right through him, dummy."

"You can?"

"Yes!"

"He looks just like old Mr. Ferguson."

"It's his ghost. Mr. Ferguson died last week, you know."

"Cripes!"

A week later I'd almost died myself, bumping into Mr. Ferguson coming out of a store. "What's wrong, son? You look like you've just seen a ghost."

A night at home alone with my sister was like being trapped in a Stephen King novel. So many ghosts, monsters, maniacs, and werewolves would show up, you would have thought they were holding a convention of things that go bump in the night. Oddly, Troll never seemed the least bit disturbed by all the phantoms flitting about. She carried on a running account of their hideous doings, much like Edward R. Murrow broadcasting radio reports of the London blitz. On one of our dark and stormy nights alone, Troll as usual was doing her spook report for my benefit. "Hear that creaky sound up in the attic? Restless human skeletons often make that sound when they—" Suddenly, she emitted a scream so filled with quavering terror that I had not the slightest doubt of its sincerity and authenticity. If ever I needed proof of the existence of actual ghosts, this was it.

"Cripes!" I thought. "This has got to be a real bad one, if it scares even a troll that much."

Actually, that is only the gist of the impression that zapped my nervous system and short-circuited my brain. That poor tormented organ was instantly rendered incapable of any thought whatsoever, let alone regulation of normal bodily functions, which were left to their own devices. Typically under such circumstances, my legs would have assumed command and propelled me home, without awaiting orders from higher authority. Since I was already home, however, they apparently became confused as to a proper route of retreat, with the result that they degenerated to a consistency somewhere between that of jelly and spaghetti al dente.

The true culprit was presently revealed to be nothing more than a mouse, which, for reasons known only to itself, had charged across the living-room floor and attempted an ascent of one of Troll's legs. I recovered my senses just in time to see the mouse ricocheting about the room, although at that point I was still unclear as to its involvement in the affair. Maybe it had seen the ghost, too. If my legs hadn't been in such bad shape, I would have joined it in ricocheting about the room.

I have always been fairly religious, not so much in my mind as in my blood and bones. It comes from being raised a Catholic. A novelist friend recently asked me whether I got my load of guilt from being Catholic. I said yes, that was it. "Where do you get your guilt from, Peter?"

"From being raised an Episcopalian."

"Ha!" I said. "You don't even know guilt!"

I spent much of my early life in the company of priests. For the most part, they regarded me less than highly, not that they should have been exceptions to the rule. I regarded them at best as nuisances and, at worst, as spoilsports. Most of them loved hunting and fishing, and our farm offered them easy access to both. They freely and frequently made use of that access. At least once a month Mom invited the parish priest out for Sunday dinner—chicken dinner. Perhaps that is why my memory tends to associate priests and chickens, no offense intended toward either.

Every spring my mother ordered a hundred or so chicks from the co-op farm store. The fluffy yellow balls arrived sometime in March, long before the outside temperature permitted putting them in one of the unheated outbuildings. To solve this problem, Mom built a pen in the unfinished upstairs of our house, carpeted it with newspaper and straw, and installed a lightbulb-heated brooder for the comfort and well-being of the chicks. Within a few weeks, the weather warmed and the chicks had developed enough to be moved outside.

One spring, however, the weather remained cold and wet well into May. As the weeks passed, the cute little yellow chicks evolved into homely little white chickens. Day by day the chickens got bigger and bigger, homelier and homelier. Busy with school, Mom had only enough time in the evening to extend the sides of the pen up to the ceiling, try to close the gaps in the chicken-wire fencing, and capture any escapees, who had spent the day exploring the nooks and crannies of the upstairs. Having cute little chicks in the house was one thing; having adolescent chickens was another. The chickens became a major embarrassment. What would the neighbors think if they knew we lived with our chickens in the house? Despite constant cleaning of the pen—my job—the upstairs began to take on the unmistakable odor of a chicken pen. And the chickens continued to grow and grow and grow.

Mom canceled all social activities at the house, and I was forbidden even to have friends over, for fear they might discover our terrible secret and broadcast it to the world: "The McManuses keep their chickens in their house!" All a playmate would have to do was open the door to the stairwell, and he would instantly hear chicken sounds drifting down, and chicken sounds were the least of what might be drifting down.

As bad luck would have it, Mom stopped to chat with

the parish priest after Mass one Sunday, and he mentioned that he hadn't been out to our place for dinner in a long while, a hint that hung heavily in the air while Mom, smiling fixedly, searched vainly for a way out. She found none.

"Oh, we'd love to have you out for dinner," she finally blurted. "How about next . . . ?"

"Today would be perfect!"

"Today. Yes, that's nice. See you this afternoon then." Smile. Smile.

Father O'Toole, a redheaded Irishman, had a particular fondness for our farm and visited it every chance he got. He was a good deal less fond of me, for what fault in his character I can't imagine. Clearly, he perceived of me as a wild and undisciplined child, and no doubt a practitioner of sins I hadn't even discovered yet. My older cousin Buck was a terrific mimic, and I eventually came to suspect him of imitating my voice at confession. I could never prove anything, even though the priest clearly viewed me as a little sinner of the first order, for whatever reason. There certainly was no sex in my life. I hadn't even heard of sex yet, although I did have the distinct feeling I was missing out on something pretty darn interesting.

It was Buck who explained the birds and the bees to me, although without reference to either. I couldn't believe it.

"Nooo!" I said. "You're pulling my leg!"

"Yeah, really, that's how it works."

"Go wahnnn! You expect me to believe that?"

"I'm tellin' ya, dummy, that's how it is."

"No way," I said, giggling. "The church wouldn't allow it."

"It *don't!*"

"So where does the stork come in, tell me that, Buck?"

"So where does the stork come in?" Buck said, mimicking me perfectly. "Gimme a break!"

"Yeah, well I bet you get a whole lot worse penances than I do, if you go around telling nasty lies like that."

"Something on the order of an Act of Contrition, an Our Father, and two hundred Hail Marys."

"Wow!" It was pretty clear Buck had a lot more fun than I did. "But I bet you're pretty embarrassed when you meet Father O'Toole outside the confessional. He can recognize your voice, you know."

"I wouldn't bet on it."

Whatever the reason, whether Buck was the problem or not, Father O'Toole simply didn't seem to believe I met his standards for young boys. On this particular day not only did I have to spend the afternoon in excruciating boredom, but Mom insisted that I try to act normal. No relief was in sight. A whole Sunday shot, and beyond that another endless week of school! Cripes!

Father O'Toole showed up for dinner fairly bursting with good humor. It was my impression that the church didn't feed priests during the week, and that they survived only on prayer and eating dinner out on Sundays, which possibly explained Father O'Toole's jolly mood.

"What's that I smell?" he roared cheerfully. "Chicken?"

"Chickens?" Mom said. "I don't smell chickens. Anybody else smell chickens?"

I thought maybe I smelled chickens, but I shook my head dutifully.

"Must be ham then," the priest said, removing his coat and tossing it over a chair.

"Oh, yes, ham it is," Mom said. "Ham for dinner. What ever was I thinking?"

Upstairs, the feathered horror pressed restlessly against the bulging sides of its prison.

Dinner moved along at the pace of a lethargic snail, with Father O'Toole occasionally looking me up and down as though trying to place me in the context of some of the sins he had heard mentioned in my voice during confessions.

"Is the boy rather advanced for his age?" he asked my mother.

"Goodness no," Mom said. "Rather the opposite. He flunked second grade. Why do you ask?"

"No reason."

About then a muffled fluttering sound came from behind the staircase door. Father O'Toole glanced idly in its direction, then turned back to his ham and the account of a strange experience that had happened to him as a young boy in Ireland.

"I was but a wee lad when the awfullest thing happened. My brother Sean came in with an injured bird he'd found in the yard, held it out for me to see, and the bird suddenly revived and flew right into my face and began to peck at me and beat me furiously about the head with its wings. Oh, it was a terrible shock! Even now that I'm a grown man, I can't stand to have a live bird near me. Constricts my throat, it does, and I break into an awful sweat. Nearly pass out, I do, like a timid wee schoolgirl in a faint. It's a dreadful burden and an awful embarrassment at times." Little did he realize that he was on the verge of one of those times. He dabbed with his napkin at a few beads of perspiration the mere telling of the story had raised on his forehead. "But I do love a nice piece of fried chicken now and again!" He led us all in a rollicking laugh, his a bit more rollicking than ours.

Another muffled fluttering sound came from behind the door. The priest glanced again in the direction of the fluttering. "What is that strange noise?"

"The wind," Mom said. "Must be a window open upstairs."

"Could be a ghost," I said, trying to be helpful. "The upstairs is haunted." The priest gave me a stern look and shook his head.

More fluttering sounds drifted out from behind the door. The women darted little puzzled worried looks at each other. Then we heard faint scratching sounds.

"I do believe you might have a rat in the house," Father O'Toole said, leaping up. "I'd better check this out."

Mom uttered a startled cry and tried to fling herself between the priest and the door. Not quick enough. Father O'Toole hurled the door wide, as if hoping to catch the rat in the act.

There, compressed, filling the doorway, was a white feathery wall of chickens, with dozens of little beaked chicken heads protruding and looking about in amazement at the wonders of the world that had suddenly been revealed to them. No less amazed was Father O'Toole, who gave a small hop, and then staggered backwards, clutching his throat and making strange gurgling sounds. Mom, too, made strange gurgling sounds. The rest of us watched in awe as the great white wall of chickens began to topple forward into the living room. A moment later, there were chickens everywhere, running and flying, chirping and squawking, a half dozen or so perched happily on the prostrate body of the priest, who had collapsed backwards stiff as a board against an overstuffed chair. As sheer spectacle, it was better than anything I could ever have imagined, my elation dampened only by the possibility that we might be held accountable for our chickens having snuffed the parish priest.

We rounded up the chickens one by one and hauled them out to the chicken house where they might freeze, but, as Mom said, that was nothing more than they deserved. Father O'Toole finally revived, and we finished dinner and even dessert without further distractions, except for blowing the occasional feather away from our plates. Mom explained how the situation arose that we had chickens in the attic, and the priest thought it all a rather good joke. By the time he left, he was once again in a jolly mood and even patted me on the head. I knew what he was thinking, though, *Better slow up, young man. Two hundred Hail Marys is a bit much for a boy your age.*

Dang that Buck!

Father O'Toole could very well have overdosed on chickens and died on the spot. No doubt he thought the birds were plotting to kill him, possibly because they had something against organized religion. Whatever he thought, he did manage to get his revenge. He owned a big old Irish setter, Butch Garrion III, who had a significantly better family tree than I did. One day Father O'Toole asked my mother if he could leave Butch at the farm for a couple of weeks. Mom said sure, the dog would be no problem. Scarcely had the priest driven off than the dog sneaked into the henhouse and killed most of the chickens. Mom was furious, possibly suspecting that the dog had been acting on orders. If that were in fact the case, the priest probably hadn't told Butch that he was being sent on a suicide mission. When Mom found most of her chickens slaughtered, she headed for the shotgun, clearly intent on turning Irish setter into Irish Stew. The only thing that stopped her, in my opinion, was the thought that killing a priest's beloved dog might result in excommunication.

Father O'Toole excused away his dog's murder spree on the grounds that Butch was merely acting on an irresistible impulse, a popular defense nowadays but rare back then. Mom would have preferred plain old vigilante justice, and during our many chickenless meals that year, I'm sure she regretted not resorting to it, even if it meant becoming a Baptist.

Just looking at a live chicken for the first time you would not suppose it was anything good to eat. This theory can be tested out. Take any two-year-old child and show him a live chicken running around pecking at bugs, and tell him, "Tonight you get to eat that thing for supper." The child will immediately fly into a screaming, crying, kicking fit. I used to run this experiment on my own children, and, until my wife, Bun, made me stop, it worked every time. A live chicken simply does not look like anything a normal person would care to eat. Suppose a fast-food restaurant kept a cage of live chickens near its entrance with a sign on the cage bragging, "This is how fresh our chicken morsels are!" That fast-food business would be sucked into oblivion quicker than you could say, "I think I'll have a Big Mac instead." Or suppose a waiter brings a live chicken to a diner's table.

"Sir, this is the chicken we'll prepare for your supper tonight, if you approve. Notice how plump and firm it is, the healthy pink of the comb, the luster of the feathers, the sparkle of the eyes."

"I'll have the prime rib."

"Very good, sir. Hey, Tony, bring in the cow!"

My point is that the typical modern eater simply does

not have the stomach for confronting his dinner eye to eye in its live state. Maybe it's the guilt thing, with people simply not wanting to share directly the responsibility for killing their own food. People get enough guilt at the office, without feeling remorse over their Chicken McNuggets. Or it could be a combination of guilt and the fact that the typical animal protein doesn't look all that appetizing in its natural state. "And these are the snails, madam, for your escargot. Notice how nice and frisky they are." Americans nowadays generally insist that their food come suitably disguised from its origins. They don't like to think of the *B* of their BLTs wallowing about in the muck of a pigpen.

It was different when I was a boy. First of all, you had a long and meaningful relationship with most of your food before you got around to, uh, breaking off the relationship. Chickens started out as cute little yellow balls of fuzz, cuteness being one of Mother Nature's major ways of protecting the young of various species. Countless puppies are rescued each year from the pound precisely because of their cuteness. A year later the rescuers are thinking, "Now, exactly why did I get this mutt, which is more trouble than the average child and just as expensive, if you count a college education?" Chickens, however, stay cute for only a couple of weeks at most, and soon reach that lanky, homely stage referred to as "spring fryers." Mom could hardly wait for her chickens to reach that stage, which, depending upon the level of our poverty in a given year, could be very early indeed. I remember wishbones so small you had to use tweezers to perform the wishing ritual.

As I mentioned previously in this report, I was a very sensitive child, and for that reason alone one might think that I would be excused from participating in the executions of chickens. I cannot even imagine saying to my four daughters, "Come on, girls, you have to help me kill a chicken for supper." Why, there would have been such shrieking and hollering and banging shut and locking of doors that surely the neighbors would have called the police to report rampant child abuse in progress. And, of course, their mother would have yelled at me, "Stop with your teasing! You'll give the girls nightmares! Don't you know how sensitive women are about such things?" To tell the truth, no.

My grandmother was the chief hatchetperson in our family, and she had absolutely no regard for my tender years or feelings. I was no more than six when I first became an accessory to one of her chicken murders. I say "murder," because the act had the necessary requirements. There was premeditation, Gram and Mom having previously planned the hit. And there was motive, namely fried chicken for supper.

"Get your nose out of that comic book," Gram ordered me. "I want you to help me kill a chicken."

"No, I hate killing stuff. Do it by yourself."

"You will, or I'll teach you a good lesson. I ain't gonna tell you twice."

"Don't you remember how I cried when that trillium died?"

Gram burst out laughing. "How could I forget! Now, I want you out here in five seconds. And I ain't gonna tell you twice."

"You already told me twice."

"Why, that's right." *Whap!* Thusly did I learn not to quibble over didactic details.

I had no choice. I knew Gram was too slow to run down one of the flighty creatures, and I, too, wanted fried chicken for supper. Gram and I walked out to the chicken pen. The chickens watched us approach, suspicion furrowing their very limited brows. "What do they want? Feeding time isn't for another three hours. This doesn't look good. That weird old lady and the kid are up to something. Watch out! The crazy old lady's got the hatchet! Run for your lives!"

There was nothing for me to do but chase down a chicken and haul it back to Gram for execution. I tried not to think about my helping her to end that chicken's dreams and desires, its hopes and aspirations, its future. Probably all we ended was its future, which, to the chicken, was probably more than enough. I doubt it was the Einstein of chickens, poised on the brink of discovering the poultry equivalent of $E=mc^2$. But who knows what mysteries lurk in the chicken mind?

Few Americans associate closely with chickens anymore, and those who do generally work in chicken factories, where their charges are scarcely more than feathered zombies. Our chickens, by contrast, ran wild and thus had the opportunity to acquire individual identities and personalities, not that it did them much good when chicken was on the supper menu. A chicken could have been tap dancing across the yard with top hat and cane, and Gram, hatchet in hand, would have ordered, "Get me Fred Astaire over there." There was one notable exception—Old Biddy. This little disheveled hen learned how to talk. When spoken to, she would respond with a chickenized impersonation of human speech, often going on at great length, presumably about the latest doings in the henhouse. Head cocked to one side, she would listen attentively as her human conversationalist responded to her gossip, and then she'd take off again on some rambling discourse. Biddy also took on the duty of protecting the family from intruders, perhaps because she had observed that my dog, Strange, ignored this responsibility, as he did all his other responsibilities. The hen started patrolling the road that led to our house. Troll once waited at home all day for a friend to come over and spend the night, but the girl never showed up. When Troll later asked her why she hadn't come over, the girl replied, "I tried to, but some stupid chicken kept attacking me and wouldn't let me walk down the road, so I went home." Old Biddy knew a criminal when she saw one.

The sketches of the characters who dominated my childhood would be incomplete without further mention of my dog, Strange. As I have written in other places, a stray dog showed up at our farm one morning wagging his tail and begging for a handout. He seemed harmless enough. My mother called him Stranger, in hope, as she said later, that he was just passing through. He stayed on for nearly fifteen years, biting the hands that fed him and criticizing my grandmother's cooking: "You expect me to eat this slop, old woman?" Gram hated the dog, although the neighbors were fond of him. No matter how bad their own dog might be, even a scruffy, smelly, barking, biting, whining, chicken-killing, egg-sucking, deer-chasing mongrel, he seemed like a regular Lassie when compared with Stranger. Mom later shortened the dog's name to Strange, which, given his character and tenure, seemed much more appropriate.

Few things shape a boy's character more than his close association with his dog. My friend Merle had a fine old dog named Bo. That's a great name for a dog, Bo. It's limited to a single syllable, so the dog doesn't have to take a course in linguistics to know that he's being called. "Here, Bo!" Merle would call. "C'mon, boy! Here, Bo!" And good old Bo would come tearing in and leap up on Merle and cover his face with kisses, his tail doing sixty wags a second from sheer happiness that his boy, his master, had called him. I'd go home and try the routine on Strange.

"Here, Strange! C'mon, boy! Here, Strange!"

Strange would stick his head out of the doghouse. "What?"

"C'mon, Strange! C'mon, boy!"

"Would you knock it off! I'm trying to get some sleep here. What a dope!" Then he'd go back to bed, muttering.

Strange was an embarrassment to the whole family. My mother gave him away once to a lonely old man who lived way back in the mountains. The man said he could use a companion. A few days later he brought Strange back, explaining that he guessed he preferred his own company. Strange watched him leave. "Crazy old fool," he said. "Cooked worse than Gram, if you can believe that!"

The best thing that could be said about Strange was that he didn't kill chickens. An intelligent dog, he apparently understood that such a crime resulted in capital punishment, after a very brief trial. He would occasionally slap a chicken around, though. "You stupid chicken, this'll teach you not to drink out of my dish! Take that! And that!" He was suspected of being on hand when Father O'Toole's dog, Butch, killed Mom's chickens, although Strange was not regarded as an actual participant. He probably stood by with his hands in his pockets and watched, though, grinning, occasionally calling out bits of advice. "There's one you missed, Butch, hiding over in the corner."

Strange regarded squirrels as terrorists, and frequently came into the house wagging and bragging that he had just saved the whole family by chasing one of them up a tree. "He was carrying a grenade," he'd say. Gram would sweep him out of the house with her broom. Strange hated my sister's big yellow tomcat, Matilda Jean, even more than he did squirrels. He also feared the cat, who would tear into him at the slightest provocation, and Strange was nothing if not provocative. Matilda Jean enjoyed lying in ambush for the dog, often on top of his house. For this reason, Strange's standard mode of leaving his house when he smelled the cat overhead was to streak out, tail tucked between his legs, jaws snapping wildly back over his shoulder. A friend who observed one of these exits, after the cat had long since sneaked off the doghouse roof, wondered aloud if maybe my dog didn't have rabies or a nervous disease of some sort. "Probably," I said. I didn't want a friend to think my dog was afraid of cats.

Despite his slovenly, cowardly, and generally despicable life, Strange died a hero's death. By then we had acquired Tippy, a happy-go-lucky dog who bounded hither and yon without a care in the world, and with no more brains than he had cares. Strange now hobbled about complaining loudly about his arthritis, Gram's cooking, Tippy, chickens, the weather, me, and just about anything else that crossed his mind. He had not improved with age. Whenever we thought he couldn't get any worse, he did, perhaps because he felt challenged to do so. He had no use for Tippy, and would have taught the young whippersnapper a good lesson for getting on his nerves, if he could have moved fast enough to catch the pup. Oddly enough, the brainless Tippy proved the undoing of Strange. One morning the sappy pup pranced out to engage in conversation one of the timber wolves our neighbors kept for watchdogs. The wolf snarled and lunged at Tippy, who immediately flipped over on his back in the traditional posture of canine submission. Tippy was dumb but no fool. This disgusting display proved too much for Strange, which was odd, because he all by himself had raised disgusting to record heights. Forgetting his arthritis, his aches and pains, his old age, and that he probably would come out second best in a fight with a squirrel, he tore into the wolf, who was at least four times his size. It was a fatal mistake. I carried the mortally wounded Strange back to the house. "I must have been out of my mind to pull a dumb stunt like that," he muttered. "Gimme a cigarette." And then he died.

Nothing improves character so much as death. I once knew a man, Pete by name, who abused his family unmercifully, stole, robbed, lied, cheated, and was suspected of at least one murder. Pete himself came to a violent end at the hands of an unknown assailant who may have been of the opinion he was performing a public service. Others thought so. Within a day of Pete's demise, however, somebody recalled a good deed the deceased had once performed, possibly an incident in which he had met a stranger on a lonely road and hadn't robbed him. Soon, even his victims were concluding that he hadn't been such a bad sort after all, merely misunderstood. Then someone recalled that the fellow had been a good worker on occasion, and someone else remembered his actually having repaid a debt. By the time of the funeral, the man's character had improved so much that he had become one of our town's leading citizens, widely revered for his acts of charity, courage, honesty, and kindness, and if he had a fun-loving tendency to pull the occasional prank, why that was to be forgiven on the grounds that nobody's perfect. Well, that was the case with Strange, too. My family and friends now remember him as a fine, upstanding dog, friendly, brave, loyal, affectionate, a dog for all seasons. "Good old Strange," they say. As for my own relationship with Strange, all I can report is that he helps explain how I got this way. If I'd had a real dog, I might have turned out differently.

In contrast to my own existence, my friends in town led orderly and peaceful lives. Their fathers worked, their mothers stayed home, they took piano lessons, did their homework, studied, got good grades, played basketball after school, went on family vacations to the seashore, mowed the lawn, got a weekly allowance, and never had chickens upstairs in their houses. I felt sorry for them, but who ever said life is fair?

From age twelve on, I ran traplines, hunted with my own shotgun, fished every spare moment, roamed wild and free in the woods and mountains, and cultivated the company of ornery old men who smelled of tobacco, whiskey, and hard living. It was nice. My friends and I often went on expeditions deep into the mountains, and it was there I first explored the fine, sweet, secret terror of wilderness and the night, and the heavy tread of Sasquatches passing near.

Some persons may find it strange that major influences on how I came to be this way consist of such mundane things as chickens and dogs and trilliums and mountain trails and lakes, with the occasional wolf or ghost passing through. I wish there were something of more significance, some great mystery to reveal, but there isn't. My family performed me a great disservice in its failure to be dysfunctional, when it had every opportunity to be so. Oh, what I could have done with that! Instead, it chose to be happy in its sublime chaos and confusion, even when we didn't know where our next meal was coming from, or sometimes worse, when we did know.

It may be, as my friend Dave surmised, that the fall on my head contributed something of significance to how I came to be this way. Ever since that *bonk*, I see everything twice. It can be a distraction, seeing everything twice, because it requires more time, and by then you're lost, or have forgotten to pick up the dry cleaning, or return home to find a strange woman cooking supper in your kitchen, or land in Baltimore when you were supposed to land in Spokane. But seeing everything twice has its advantages. When I return from an outing with friends and report to our wives what happened, my friends think they have been on a different trip. "I don't remember it like that," they say. "Is that how it happened?" Of course that's the way it happened, if you see everything twice. Their problem is, they see everything only once. It's a pity. And it's just a darn good thing they have me along to tell them how it was. Otherwise, they would miss out on so much.

Ethics, and What to Do About Them

Today's lecture is on ethics, with special emphasis on situational ethics as opposed to regular ethics. As you no doubt are aware, situational ethics differ considerably from regular ethics, which prescribe such old-fashioned restraints on human behavior as Don't steal, Don't lie, Don't cheat, and so on. You can see how confining regular ethics are. Situational ethics, on the other hand, are much less confining and therefore more fun.

If you don't know which brand of ethics you are operating under, here is a little test. Simply ask yourself if your behavior is as good when you're alone as it would be if a bunch of blabbermouthed witnesses were present. Okay, so you flunked. Don't worry about it. Almost everyone flunks that test, except for Extremely Boring People, who enjoy displaying their honesty by confessing every tiny indiscretion.

Boring Person to Grocery Clerk: "I must tell you that I

ate a grape in the produce department and wish to be charged for it."

Clerk: "That's very honest of you to tell me that. Not many people *yawnnnn* are so honest nowadays. Because you are so honest, the grape's on us."

Boring Person: "But I insist! I just wouldn't feel right if I didn't pay for that grape."

Clerk: "Oh, all right. What kind of grape was it, concord or green seedless or red seedless? They're all a different price per pound."

Boring Person: "Green seedless I think. I know it was green but it may have been a red seedless that wasn't ripe. How many red seedless grapes in a pound? Are there more in a pound than—"

At this point, Next Person In Checkout Line tries to stuff a *National Enquirer* down Boring Person's throat, thereby demonstrating one of the flaws in excessively ethical behavior.

A less rigorous test of your own ethics is simply to ask yourself if what you are doing might be featured as a hidden-camera investigation on "60 Minutes" or "20/20." This standard leaves you free to pilfer the occasional grape in the produce department but limits your ethical behavior to acts that don't result in, as the ethics scholars phrase it, "hard time."

Let us now consider a few situational-ethics situations.

Situation: Suppose you are out fishing with the president of your company, and he catches and keeps one trout more than his limit. You have caught and kept one less trout than your limit. Both of you simultaneously notice a game warden approaching. Your company president gives you a wink and slips his extra trout into your creel. You each now have a legal limit in your creel.

What is ethical in this situation? The answer is obvious. You should explain to the game warden that your company president caught one more trout than the limit and slipped it into your creel. Furthermore, you should insist that the president be ticketed for the violation.

That is the ethical response, however, only if you are the chairman of the board, own more than 50 percent of the stock in the company, or are independently wealthy. On the other hand, if you are only an executive vice-president with a family to support and a large mortgage, such a response is described by French ethics scholars as *très bête* or, as we say in English, "really stupid, you idiot, particularly in this economy and with middle-management job opportunities being what they are!"

Thusly does the appropriate situational-ethics response depend upon the particular situation.

Situation: Suppose you are mountain climbing and your partner, with whom you are roped together, slips and falls. He jerks you into space with him. The two of you are suspended from the rope, with him on the bottom end. You could climb up the rope, but you can't climb up dragging your partner behind you. If you cut the rope beneath you, your partner falls. If you don't cut the rope, both of you will freeze to death. The ethical question: Should you cut the rope and save yourself, even as your partner watches in horror, or should you say, "Hey, look, Fred, a bald eagle!"

Under boring old ethics, honesty is absolute. That is to say, it is no more dishonest to steal a pencil from your employer than it is a million dollars, even though the theft of a pencil is easier in that it doesn't usually require a valid passport and some fluency in a foreign language. Many people go through life considering themselves honest, all the while knowing that they have stolen countless pencils and paper clips from their employer. But what is the difference between them and the people who have stolen a million dollars, except the latter have a much better tan?

If asked, most people would probably say that the thing of ultimate value in the world is human life. Let us suppose, then, that the hypothetical situation arises in which you know with absolute certainty that you can save the life of some mean and nasty stranger on the other side of the globe merely by walking down Main Street at high noon without a stitch of clothes on, and without benefit of first losing fifty pounds and working out in the gym for six months. The only consequences to you will be a few minutes of stark-naked embarrassment, and, of course, listening to the story told at hunting camp for the rest of your days. In exchange for those minor inconveniences, you will save the mean and nasty person's life. The ethical question: Should you send flowers or only a card expressing condolences?

Situation: As a young boy, George Washington was asked by his father if he knew who had chopped down the cherry tree. "I cannot tell a lie," replied George. "It was I, Father. I did it with my little hatchet." Ethical question: Because George obviously realized his father wouldn't consider him only one of several possible suspects, why hadn't he prepared a suitable alibi before he chopped down the cherry tree? ("About three o'clock this afternoon, Father, I noticed that my little hatchet was missing and . . .")

Situation: A Girl Scout mistakenly sells you two boxes of peanut butter cookies for the price of one. Ethical question:

Should you keep both boxes or exchange one for chocolate chip?

Situation: You are hiking in the mountains with your best friend, when he is suddenly attacked by a bear. Ethical question: Should you instantly flee back down the trail while the bear is occupied, or should you pause long enough to ask your friend to toss you the car keys?

Situation: A neighbor shows up at your door with a pail of morel mushrooms and asks if they are safe to eat. Ethical question: Do you tell him the mushrooms in the pail are referred to as the Sudden Death Morel and offer to dispose of them for him, or do you tell him they are not only edible but delicious and never fatal, unless, of course, consumed by a person who sometime in his life has eaten pasta, which, as it happens, you haven't?

Situation: You are headed down to the store to buy a lottery ticket. Your best friend, who is still recovering from the bear attack, gives you a dollar and asks you to buy him a ticket, too. You purchase the tickets, stick them in your billfold, and then forget about them. A couple of weeks after the drawing, you remember the tickets and discover that one of them is the winner of $15 million. Ethical question: Should you tell your friend about your sudden inheritance of your uncle's fortune or should you share your winnings, possibly by buying him a really nice rod-and-reel combination?

Situation: Honest Abe Lincoln discovers that a shopkeeper has mistakenly given him a dollar more in change than Abe was entitled to. Abe walks twenty miles to return the dollar and then walks twenty miles home again. Ethical question: How did a guy like this get to be president, anyway?

Situation: You and your friend Burt are in a spike camp high up in the mountains when you become snowbound because of a blizzard. After two weeks of being crowded together in the tiny tent, you are both cold and starving and becoming desperate. Ethical question: Is it permissible to kill Burt to stop him from doing his John Wayne impressions?

Situation: You and your best friend are far out in the ocean in a small boat. There is only one life jacket in the boat. The boat begins to sink. That is when you notice that your best friend is grinning and already wearing the life jacket. Ethical question: Will your best friend forget that business with the bear and accept $15 million for the life jacket?

That completes this lecture on situational ethics. Now, to see if you have been paying attention, there will be a pop quiz. No cheating! I'm sorry about that, but I still suffer from a bad case of old-fashioned ethics. It has been a real problem for me socially and financially, but I expect that sometime soon scientists will come up with a pill for it. I just wish they'd hurry.

Bambo

I HAVE LONG been fascinated by the idea of convergence. You yourself, for example, are a product of convergence, and it won't do you any good to deny it. Although you may be of the impression that you have been around only since, let's say, July 10, 1946, the fact is that you've been around ever since the world began and even before that. Back at the beginning of time, you were scattered in tiny bits all over the place, and didn't seem to have a whole lot of career prospects. Sure, you say, you often feel that way nowadays, but back then you were only these randomly isolated quark-size bits. So millions and even billions and trillions of years ago, all these bits began to converge on a pinprick dot in time, July 10, 1946. And suddenly, at that moment, all the little pieces came together as the integrated you. Isn't that marvelous? Just think of all the thousands of people your little bits and pieces traveled through to become you, although I wouldn't dwell too hard on that aspect, no sirree, bub.

Unfortunately, you no sooner get it all together after all those billions of years of converging through time and space then what happens—you start falling apart. Your bits start dispersing, often in big chunks. Hardly seems worth all the trouble, does it?

So what has convergence to do with hunting and fishing? Absolutely everything, that's what. If you'll just shut up and stop complaining, I'll elucidate. The whole object of hunting and fishing is to converge on the same point in space and time as your fish or game. Through great effort—and I hope you appreciate this—I have worked out a computer model of my typical deer hunt. Not only does this model show the sequence of my movements through the hunt, it shows the simultaneous movements of My Deer, a creature my computer refers to as Bambo.

Keep in mind that we are talking about convergence here, and the point of this scientific treatise is to demonstrate how Bambo and I, apparently through random activity, or chaos, converge on the same point in space and time. Here goes:

I'm lying in bed peacefully asleep. Bambo, thirty miles away, happily grazes with a couple dozen of his associates on a crop of alfalfa a rancher is depending on to keep him from joining the ranks of the homeless.

By the way, at the risk of alarming the reader with the suspicion that I am one of those geezers who start off with a brief and simple report and then stretch it to infinity with endless digressions, I must make this observation about the feeding habits of deer. From time to time, I read some nonsense about deer being browsers, not grazers. The truth is that deer enjoy browsing only on fruit trees you have nurtured through a couple of years of heat and cold to the point where they are about to bear fruit. If you planted a fruit tree on top of your garage roof, deer would find a ladder and climb up on the roof in order to browse on your tree. This is a well-documented fact. Once they have browsed your fruit trees down to nubbins, the deer will then go back to their efforts to induct the rancher into the legions of the homeless.

Now, where was I? Ah yes, I'm asleep in my bed, while Bambo munches away on the rancher's alfalfa.

My alarm goes off. I jerk awake and thrash about in the dark, trying to punch off the alarm, which I am of the immediate impression is some kind of vile practical joke. At the very same moment, Bambo lifts his head and glances around. He senses something, even over a distance of thirty miles. Indeed, it is as if he too has heard my alarm. "Rather early for Pat to be getting up," he muses. "That rascal must be going hunting. This could be good!"

Head still clogged with the residue of sleep, I start pulling on my hunting clothes. I ask my wife, Bun, "What's for breakfast?" From the lack of response and the fact that she has a pillow clamped over her head, I deduce that it will be weak coffee and stale donuts from the Quick Stop Gas & Grocery. I grab my rifle and hunting gear and stumble out through the dark to Retch Sweeney's pickup truck, where I find Retch dozing with his head resting on the steering wheel.

Sensing that he is at extreme risk, Bambo turns and saunters toward his resident mountaintop, taking great care to conceal the terror quivering just beneath the surface of his hairy hide. Crossing the very road Retch and I will be traversing two hours later, he pauses a moment to leave a rudimentary sign for Retch and me, possibly as a crude commentary on our character. He then slips gracefully into a seemingly impenetrable thicket and strolls up a steep and meandering game trail a mile or so to his favorite ridge on the mountain. He beds down under a picturesque old gnarled pine on the point of the ridge, a position that gives him a clear view of any adversary approaching from below. A night of debauchery has left him a bit weary, so he decides to take a snooze.

As Bambo drifts off to sleep, Retch and I pull out of Quick Stop Gas & Grocery with our coffee and donuts.

"Hey boy, I feel lucky today!" Retch tells me. "I've got a game plan all worked out. Man, this plan is perfect. To be a successful deer hunter, you've got to think like a deer. And I think like a deer!"

"Which may explain why you flunked algebra," I reply.

"Deer hunting has nothing to do with algebra. It has to do with geometry. It is a matter of intersecting lines." He steers with one hand, while drawing out his plan on the dust of the dashboard. "This here is Misery Ridge. My deer is here, a big old six-point buck. I move up the ridge like this. He senses me and decides to escape to Mount Horrible. I drop over this saddle. Our two lines of travel intersect at this point. And *bang!* I've got my deer. Simple as that. Plane geometry."

"You flunked geometry too, remember?" I say. "And it's easy to see why. Besides, deer hunting has nothing to do with geometry. It is a matter of convergence. It's like an automobile accident. You are driving around town at the same time another person is driving around town. Now even though you are both meandering randomly all over town, you are still converging on the same point in space and time. *Crash!* You can retrace the movements of any two drivers involved in an accident and see that it was inevitable. If either of them had made a wrong turn, been delayed by a stoplight, or left home one minute earlier or later, the accident wouldn't have happened. It is the same with deer hunting. Any hunt appears to contain an infinite number of variables, but all of these are controlled by the unifying principle of convergence. Within the apparent randomness of chaos, there is a clearly defined order, and—"

"Stop!" cries Retch. "You're giving me a headache!"

"No doubt. Here I try to hold an intelligent conversation with you and . . . Hey, what happened to my other donut?"

"I randomly ate it. The donut and I converged on each other at the same point in space and time. Ha!"

"Very funny."

Retch and I are rattling along a dirt road. High on the mountain above us, Bambo lifts his head and cocks his ears.

"Hey, stop and back up," I tell Retch. "I think I saw some deer sign back there on the road. Yes, there it is. And look at the size of those tracks! I have a strong sense that if I follow those tracks up the mountain, the deer and I will experience a moment of convergence."

"Yeah, right. Well, I'm heading up to Misery Ridge to intersect my deer on his line of retreat. Simple geometry."

"Convergence!"

"Geometry!"

I get out of the truck, ease the door shut, slip across the road, up the steep bank, and force my way into the thicket. High up on the mountain, Bambo listens intently. He detects the sound of air forcibly expelled from a set of lungs, a loud *Oof!* The thicket has repelled me, flinging me flat on my back on the road below. I get up and dust myself off. "So, that's the way you want to play," I say to the thicket, which smugly chooses not to respond. I climb back up the bank and slide gracefully into the deer trail.

Often, the only way to move through thick brush is to traverse the three-foot-high tunnels deer have burrowed through it. The procedure consists of bending your knees into a half crouch and extending your torso out from the hips so that it is parallel to and approximately three feet from the ground. Employing this posture, which approximates the shape of the letter Z, you can move unrestricted through the densest of brush for several hundred yards, pausing only occasionally to catch your breath and to emit a hushed but long, quavering scream of anguish. Catching your breath is optional. The scream, however, should be executed at regular intervals, because if you let it build up into one big scream, it will not be hushed and will frighten not only all game but some of the other hunters off the mountain.

I emerge from the thicket. Curious, Bambo stretches out his neck to check the terrain far below. He has detected four hushed screams at regular intervals. "Aha," he thinks. "Pat has survived the thicket. Now, he has to work his way around the sheer precipice. That will take him at least an hour. Even he is not stupid enough to climb the precipice."

· Halfway up the precipice, I pause on a quarter-inch ledge to plan my next move. Immediately above me is an overhang, requiring me to leap out and up and grab it by its upper edge and raise myself to the lip of rock, where I can get a new handhold by hanging momentarily by my chin. After that comes the tricky part of the climb. By the time I reach the top of the precipice, I am totally tuckered out.

Bambo peers down from his ridge. He can see me now. Instantly alert to the impending peril, he yawns, whisks some flies off his back, and rests his chin on a log the better to keep an eye on me.

I circle around Bambo's ridge and drop over the far side of the mountain. Shaken to the core by his narrow escape, Bambo goes back to sleep.

Six hours later, with darkness closing in, I arrive at the prearranged rendezvous with Retch. He is sitting on the hood of the truck while he finishes off my lunch.

"I figured you was lost and that I'd better eat your lunch so I'd have enough energy to rush off and organize a search team," he explains.

"Very considerate of you."

"I see you didn't converge with your deer."

I unload my rifle and put it in the cab of the truck. "True. But I notice you didn't intersect with your deer."

"My deer is a little weak on his geometry."

"He's not the only one," I say. "Well, I'm going to stick to my theory about . . ."

Bambo walks out of a thicket twenty yards away. He stops in the middle of the road and stares at me. I stare back. We exchange rudimentary signs. He then sidles off toward the rancher's alfalfa field.

". . . convergence."

Retch, a dill pickle hanging from his mouth, watches Bambo recede into the night. "Big deal."

Get Ready

I HAVE NEVER been a great devotee of preparation, choosing instead to wing it. Various enterprises of mine, sporting and otherwise, no doubt would profit from a bit of preparation, but at the loss of spontaneity, not to mention the exhilaration that comes from being caught short in dire circumstances. This is to say nothing of the fine cardiovascular benefits to be gained. For example, I once discovered on a night trip through the mountains that the distance was twenty miles longer than my gas supply. Preparation for the trip would have required me to flip a switch to check the fuel level in the truck's auxiliary fuel tank. And flipping switches can be so tedious. Half one's life nowadays is spent flipping switches.

So there I was, bumping along through the night in a wild and remote region populated only by the occasional family of Sasquatches and a few space aliens awaiting a lone traveler on whom to run weird and painful experiments. Throw in a homicidal maniac or two. The demographics of the region didn't occur to me, of course, until I exhausted the fuel of the first tank and calmly switched over to the reserve tank, which was *bone dry!*

Now is when the cardiovascular and overall health benefits kicked in. As is my practice on such occasions, I stepped out of my vehicle and began performing hop-aerobics while pounding on the hood of the truck with both fists, thereby exercising both my upper and lower body, my heart and lungs, and even my vocal cords. Particularly my vocal cords.

The following morning I emerged on foot from the mountains full of vim and vigor and the mental alertness that comes from having hiked twenty miles and also from having outrun a carnivorous Sasquatch who made the mistake of clumsily stepping on a dry twig while trying to sneak up on me. My lack of preparation had provided me with yet another inspirational and invigorating adventure that I might otherwise have missed, had I subjected myself to the tedium of preparation.

I suspect it was my disregard for preparation that led to my distinguished career in the Boy Scouts, whose motto is, as you know, "Be Prepared." If I'm not mistaken, I still hold the record for longest period in the rank of Second-class Scout—five years! I would think the Boy Scouts of America at the very least would have awarded me a plaque in recognition of this singular achievement, but they have not. Indeed, I suspect there has been an effort in the organization to erase all evidence of my ever having been a scout. All I have to say to them in that regard is, "Just don't expect me to help any little old ladies across the street!"

It was not unusual for me to arrive at camp cookouts

with nothing to cook out. Had I prepared for the cookout by reading the little mimeographed set of instructions for the outing, I would have learned that we were supposed to bring our own food, which struck me as odd, because on all previous outings we were supposed to bring our own food. This predicament forced me to live off the land, by which I mean visiting the campsites of several Cub Scouts who happened to be along.

"Hi, Melvin. Hope you're enjoying your first cookout. And what are you burning on the end of your stick there? Ah, a wienie. Always a good choice. Oh, my gosh! That stick you're using is a highly poisonous willow! Good thing for you I happened to stop by. What you were about to dine on, Melvin, is known as the Two-step Death Wienie. After your first bite, you're dead before you can take more than two steps. Didn't know that, hunh? Well, give me the wienie, and I'll take it off in the woods and dispose of it properly. Better hand me one of those buns to wrap it in, Melvin, because touching it with my bare hands could be fatal. Now, go wash your own hands thoroughly and get another kind of stick. And don't let this happen again, Scout, because next time I may not be there to save you."

My wife, Bun, is a preparation fanatic. A week before any trip she has all her bags packed and ready to go. Then she unpacks and repacks them two or three times, just to make sure she hasn't forgotten anything.

"You'd better get packed," she tells me.

I chuckle. "Are you kidding me or what? It's three days before we have to leave."

Two days later, she yells at me, "You'd better get packed!"

"Calm down. We don't leave until tomorrow."

On the day we are to leave, she screams, *"Get packed!"*

"Don't rush me. It's a good two hours before the plane leaves."

My packing for a trip consists of grabbing an armful of clothes out of the closet and stuffing them in a suitcase. It's fast and efficient and requires absolutely no preparation. Oh sure, maybe I do occasionally show up at a black-tie dinner wearing a yellow tie and a denim jacket. The combination helps me avoid a lot of boring small talk with the other guests.

Lately, though, I do make sure to bring my own underwear. It's not that Bun's panty hose are particularly uncomfortable, slippery though they may be, but there's always the worry I'll trip on some stairs and be rushed off to an emergency room:

"These panty hose aren't actually mine, Nurse."

"Yeah, right."

My rich and sophisticated friend Parker Whitney is another preparation fanatic. His checklist for a weekend camping trip is the size of an unabridged dictionary. Parker prepares for every contingency known to man or woman. If he's traveling in the Arctic and a rattlesnake shows up during a blizzard and bites someone, Parker will be prepared to whip out his snake-bite kit and treat the victim on the spot. If a log rolls onto a person's legs during a backpacking excursion, Parker will produce a two-ton hydraulic jack from his tidy pack. "You never know," is his motto. My lack of preparation, of course, used to drive Parker crazy.

"What?" he'd screech. "No, I will not let you use my toothbrush just because you forgot yours. I do, however, have several emergency spare toothbrushes, one of which I will sell you for twenty-five dollars cash, the purpose of the exorbitant price being to teach you a lesson."

"I've got you there, Parker. I forgot to bring any money with me. Ha!"

"In that case, you'll just have to do without brushing your teeth. No money, no toothbrush."

"You leave me with no choice but to breathe on you."

"Take the toothbrush."

That is what I mean by winging it. Almost any problem caused by lack of preparation can be solved with a little ingenuity. Nowadays, however, I am seldom forced to use drastic threats. Over the years, my camping companions, for example, have been conditioned to prepare for my lack of preparation. They now bring along an extra set of anything they think I might leave at home, which is usually just about everything.

Thusly does lack of preparation save me enormous amounts of time and energy that I can apply to more enjoyable endeavors. Even Parker Whitney, one of the last holdouts, has begun to show signs of succumbing to my efforts to condition him. Take a recent camping trip for example.

"I've noticed that the only thing you've brought on our last couple of camping trips was your hat," Parker said, as I climbed into his well-stocked vehicle.

"I'm glad you noticed that, Parker," I replied. "I trust you are now adequately prepared with double sets of everything. Also, as you no doubt recall, last time you forgot my favorite brand of orange marmalade, offering up the flimsy excuse that you cannot stand orange marmalade yourself. I really don't like to call attention to a fellow camper's lack of preparation, but I find that sort of negligence reprehensible."

"I'm sorry," Parker replied. "Forgetting the orange marmalade was inexcusable. I don't know what I could have been thinking of. This time I brought half a case of the dreadful stuff."

"Good. Now, there's just one other thing."

"I suppose you are referring to the fact that this time you have forgotten even your hat. In preparation for just such an event, I've brought along a couple extra hats."

"Excellent, Parker! But I hadn't realized until now that I had forgotten my hat."

"So what's the problem?"

"Nothing serious I expect. I doubt you're the sort of chap who would go about in panty hose, are you old boy?"

Toe

I WAS CONTEMPLATING my toes this morning and—I know this will interest you—the big toe on my right foot is almost back to normal. It has taken nearly a full year for the blackened toenail to grow out and be replaced by a shiny pink new nail. My big toe, aside from a slightly flattened shape, looks every bit as good as its associates: the piggy who stayed home, the piggy who had roast beef, the piggy who had none, and the piggy who went "wee weee weeee" all the way home. Actually, that last little piggy didn't say anything. It was I who went *"Wee weee weeeee!"* all the way home.

I flattened the toe during my Annual Major Nerve-Wracking Spring Building Project. My wife, Bun, likes to claim I start off pursuing my Annual Nerve-Wracking Spring Building Project and end up with it pursuing me. Okay, sure, there was the project last year, the one recorded in the blackened nail of my big toe, but that's certainly the exception, if you don't count my pouring the concrete walk (May 1972), putting a new porch on the cabin (May 1981), installing a deer fence around the garden (May 1985), and building a cedar-strip canoe (May 1986–19   ). Even though those building projects may have pursued me in the end, they never actually caught me. If you can't escape from one of your own building projects, don't call yourself a handyman.

"Time I got started building a new dock," I said to Bun over breakfast one morning last June. "Got to get it done before the river starts to rise. If I wait any longer, I'll have to wear *scuba* gear! Ha ha!"

"I'd better order the *scuba* gear right away," Bun said.

"I was only kidding. It'll be another three weeks before the river starts coming up. I'll have this dock done long before then."

"One air tank or two?"

I flew into action right after breakfast. I called my friend Mike, a logger, and asked him if he could get me twelve cedar poles to use for pilings. No problem, he said, and the very next morning he hauled in the poles, each one twelve feet long and about eight inches in diameter. Mike casually tossed them off the back of his pickup truck and into my driveway. I was pleased to see they were so light, because that would make them easy for me to carry down to the dock site.

I invited Mike in for a cup of coffee. "Watch your step," I told him as we headed for the house.

"You really should have a concrete walk put in," Mike said.

"This *is* a concrete walk," I said. "Poured it myself back in seventy-two."

"I see," he said. "I didn't know that."

"Yes, I did the whole walk all by myself."

"It's very interesting."

"Thanks."

We got our coffee and some little round donut holes and brought them out to the porch. Mike dropped one of the donut holes and before he could pick it up it rolled across the porch and off the edge.

"I built the porch to be self-cleaning," I said. "That's why it slants the way it does."

"Good idea," Mike said. "By the way, I was wondering why you have that deer penned up in your garden."

"He's not penned up," I said. "He comes and goes through that fence as he pleases. That's why we call it a deer fence."

"Oh, I thought for a moment it was a cage of some sort, like that one over there. Pretty nice cage."

"Cedar-strip canoe."

"Of course. I really have to get my eyes checked. Can't see worth a darn anymore. So, who are you having build this dock for you?"

"Nobody. Building it myself. This may surprise you, Mike, but I'm pretty handy with tools."

After Mike left, I went down to the riverbank and marked out a nice big rectangle, and drove in a stake to mark the position of each of the twelve pilings. I hate a puny dock. All my neighbors have little insignificant docks. This one would be big enough to hold square dances on.

My first effort at digging a piling hole in loose rock didn't turn out well. The sides kept caving in, and by the time I had it deep enough, the hole was the size of a bomb crater. I then went up to haul the first pole down from the driveway, and discovered that dew had soaked into it and tripled its weight since Mike had tossed it off the truck. Still, I wrestled it up onto my right shoulder and by running sideways at a precarious tilt managed to get the pole down to the hole before I toppled over. After the piling was set and solidly tamped in, a process that took scarcely more than six hours —do you realize how much gravel needs to be shoveled to fill a bomb crater?—I came to a sudden realization: my neighbors might be offended if I built a dock twice the size of theirs. They would think I was showing off, maybe even trying to embarrass them. It would be much more neighborly on my part if I built a dock with only eight pilings.

After I had set three pilings, it became clear to me that the neighbors would be even more appreciative if my dock were actually smaller than theirs. Six pilings would be plenty. Four would serve. It was as I prepared to set the final piling that the incident of the big toe occurred. Hugging the pole vertically to my chest, I staggered to the edge of the excavation, at which moment the gravel under my feet caved in. I shot to the bottom of the hole, as did the piling, which might have split in two from the impact, had it not been cushioned by my big toe.

Bun came running out of the house. "I just saw a log fly by the window!" she yelled. "What on earth is going on out here!"

"Nothing," I growled.

"Something is," she said. "First the log flies by the window, and then I hear something go 'wee weeee weeeee'!"

Much to everyone's surprise, I had the dock finished before the river came up. It is a modest dock, too small for square dances but plenty big enough for tap dancing.

While I was contemplating my toes this morning, it occurred to me that people in general seem to find mashing a toe amusing, so long as it isn't their toe. I don't recall receiving a bit of sympathy for flattening my toe into approximately the size and shape of a Ping-Pong paddle. In fact, my so-called friends and associates burst into loud guffaws upon hearing I had dropped a 300-pound log on it. Disgusting! But I, alas, am no better than they.

I had been installing a simple built-in cabinet in my upstairs office. One thing led to another, and pretty soon a wall had to be replaced, along with a few odds and ends related to the structural supports. Bun, fearing that the upstairs office might soon be in the downstairs living room, insisted that I bring in a carpenter. She then took to bed with a sick headache. (Women simply don't have the nerves for watching a home handyman ply his craft.) So I let my bandaged fingers do some walking through the Yellow Pages and found a carpenter by the name of Big Earl. I called him.

"Your office is on the second floor?" he said.

"At the moment," I said. "I would appreciate it if you could get out here as soon as possible."

"That means I'll have to carry lumber upstairs. The problem is, mister, I mashed my big toe the other day and it's all swoll up something awful and hurts like the very dickens."

I managed to ease the pain in Big Earl's toe with the offer to apply large amounts of cash to the palm of his hand. Scarcely had I hung up the phone than Big Earl knocked at my door. With one foot in a boot and the other in a loose-fitting slipper, he hobbled into the kitchen, wincing sufficiently at every step that I suspected an even greater application of cash to palm might be needed to soothe his suffering.

Big Earl checked out the situation in the office and said the first order of business would be to haul some lumber up the stairs. I explained that we would have to be quiet, because my wife was in bed with a sick headache. Big Earl said he would take eleven sick headaches in exchange for a mashed toe.

As we were carrying a sheet of three-quarter-inch plywood up the stairs, each of us grasping an end, I heard a slight bump. Not realizing that Big Earl had thumped his sore toe on the top step, I thought for a moment he had burst out in a crude attempt at yodeling. I tried to shush him, fearing he would disturb Bun. Distracted by what up to that moment he considered to be a major pain in his toe, Big Earl allowed the sheet of plywood to slip from his fingers. It is common knowledge among handymen that a sore toe acts as a magnet to any heavy object dropped within twenty feet of it. So even though Big Earl had nine other perfectly good toes for the corner of the plywood to land on, the heavy sheet zeroed in and landed with a spongy thud on the previously injured toe.

Big Earl shot straight into the air. By the time he came down, he had flung off the slipper, grabbed up the foot containing the damaged party, and clutched it to his midsection. No sooner had he landed than he bounded off in a series of sprightly one-legged hops, all the more remarkable for a man of his size and age. In mere seconds he explored all the rooms on the second floor and had started retracing his route. At one point he hopped in and out of the bedroom where Bun was lying down with a cold cloth on her head. A moment later, she looked out into the hall, but by then Big Earl had vanished into the office.

"I must be having a migraine," she mumbled and went back to bed.

Each time Big Earl hopped by me, I tried to engage him in casual conversation, but he showed little interest. Indeed, he hadn't uttered a sound during the whole event, except for his aborted attempt at a yodel. Finally, he hopped down the stairs and out of the house. I followed along behind, carrying his slipper and trying to comfort him.

"Mashed toes do smart some, don't they, Big Earl? I wouldn't worry about it, though. I doubt your toe is broken. I mashed my big toe with a three-hundred-pound piling last spring. Boy, just be glad it was only a sheet of plywood that hit your toe. You take a three-hundred-pound piling, now that hurts!"

Uncomforted, Big Earl hopped into his pickup and drove off without saying a word. He must have been nearly a half mile away when I heard him make his first utterance: *"WEEE WEEEE WEEEEE WEEEEEE!"* Now there was something to which I could relate.

As I say, there is something about toes that is inherently amusing. It is not unusual for a normally sensitive and sympathetic person like myself to burst out in maniacally wild laughter at the mere thought of somebody else bashing a toe. So I am happy to report that with considerable difficulty I remained grimly solemn during and for days after the event, an attitude I achieved by refusing to think about the madly hopping Big Earl. If someone so much as mentioned the word *toe* or *hop,* my lips would quiver into a smile, but I would fight off the smile and return to strained solemnity. I think it totally reprehensible to find amusement in the suffering of another human being, even when it concerns only a big toe. To do so clearly reveals a major flaw in one's character, particularly when one feels an uncontrollable urge to burst into crazed laughter every time he recalls the incident. The trick, of course, is simply not to recall the incident.

Unfortunately, it was while I was seated in a crowded movie theater the following week that the image of the hopping Big Earl suddenly and without warning leaped vividly into my head. I only wish it hadn't occurred during the scene in which the poor little blind girl learns that her faithful seeing-eye dog, Rex, has just been flattened by a steamroller.

The Bandage

I HURT MY hand the other day and am happy to report that the bandage is impressive. There's not much use getting hurt if it doesn't result in a significant bandage. The minute I got the bandage on, I rushed down to Kelly's Bar & Grill. Fortunately, most of the Kelly Irregulars were in attendance.

"There's ol' Pat. Yo, Pat! Haven't seen you in a while. Been fishin'?"

"Caught it in a piece of machinery," I said matter-of-factly. I loved saying that. Made it sound as if I do real work. Most of the guys at Kelly's do real work, run machines of some sort—logging trucks, skidders, Cats, backhoes, loaders, forklifts, chain saws. They're always getting hurt, guys like Lefty, Stumpy, Popeye, Toeless Joe, and Mel. Sometimes they aren't lucky enough to get a big bandage, so nobody believes they've been hurt. A tree bonked Mel on the head, and he didn't get so much as a Band-Aid. Nevertheless, the doctors in the emergency room got all excited when they saw that Mel's head sat flat on his shoulders, like a pumpkin on a fence. They scheduled him for immediate surgery, apparently to extract his neck, but then someone told them Mel's head has always sat flat on his shoulders. The doctors had just assumed that Mel was a cowboy, not even guessing it was the bonk on the head that bowed his legs out and popped his kneecaps. That's what Mel said, anyway. He was pretty darn upset, too, that he didn't get a bandage.

"I caught a few up on the West Branch the other morning," Stumpy responded.

"Yeah, I was running a sod-cutter at the time," I explained.

"Mostly rainbows," Stumpy said. "A couple of cutthroat."

"Wicked machine, those sod-cutters," I said. "Luckily, I have quick reflexes. Otherwise might have lost my arm."

"Mostly ten-inchers," Stumpy said. "I did get one rainbow about fourteen."

It finally became apparent that nothing would do but that I satisfy the curiosity about my bandage by telling the whole story.

Yes, indeed, sod-cutters are wicked machines, at least the one I rented from Stuff Rentals. Jake Stuff, the owner, was out trying to hunt down a backhoe that hadn't been returned, and had left his boy, Henry, to run the shop alone. Henry has his heart set on being a professional tournament golfer, but since he's already about thirty-five, I don't think he's going to make it. In my opinion, though, he would certainly make a much better golf pro than a tool-rental person.

Henry took me out to the storage shed and showed me the sod-cutter, which looked something like a cultivator—a mean cultivator. "There it is," he said, nodding at it, his hands resting under the bib of his overalls.

"How do you make it go?" I asked.

"Beats me," Henry said. "Ain't never run it."

"You got the manual?"

"Nope."

"I can probably figure it out when I get home," I said. "I'm pretty good with machines."

I got the sod-cutter home and unloaded it by rolling it down a couple of narrow planks, reaching a top speed of about thirty-five miles per hour between the pickup bed and the ground. Unloading a heavy piece of rental equipment single-handedly from a pickup would make a good daredevil act for a circus: "And now, in the center ring, ladies and gentlemen, Pat McManus will single-handedly, for the first time, attempt to unload a 500-pound sod-cutter from the bed of his pickup by running it down two narrow planks!" Drumroll. Screams. Applause. Actually, the screams came from my wife, Bun, and the applause from my irascible next-door neighbor, Al Finley, the banker, who was peering over our adjoining fence.

"What now?" Finley demanded irritably. "It looks as if you're intent on disturbing the peace and quiet of the whole neighborhood."

"You don't recognize a sod-cutter when you see one, Finley? Well, this here is a major industrial machine."

"What's it do, besides make a horrible racket?"

"It cuts sod, of course. Bun wants me to dig up the sod along the fence there so she can put in a flower garden. This machine will do the job in one-tenth the time it would take me to dig up all that sod by hand."

"You don't know anything about running equipment

like that," Finley said. "I'd better go call nine-one-one right now and have them start the ambulance on its way. Or the SWAT team!"

"Very funny," I said. I squatted down and studied the warning printed on the side of the sod-cutter, which stated that I was supposed to pull levers A and B before starting the motor. There were about twelve levers in sight, so I assumed that the biggest and next biggest had to be A and B. I pulled them.

At about that moment, across town, Jake Stuff arrived back at the rental shop and asked where the sod-cutter was. Henry said it was out. "You rented out the sod-cutter? You idgit! Don't you know there's no way to shut that monster off, except by shorting out the electrical system with a screwdriver!"

"Yup. But the fella said he knew machines. I 'spect he can figure that out for himself. Here's his name right here on the rental contract."

"*Him?* Good gosh a-mighty, he don't know nothin' about machines!" Jake jumped in his pickup and headed for my place.

Even as Jake was speaking ill of my knowledge of machines, I was reaching for the pull-cord to start the engine.

"I'd prefer you didn't have that monster aimed right at my fence," Finley said. "Turn it in another direction."

"Don't be silly, Finley. It's too heavy to turn without the motor going. Besides, this sod-cutter won't budge an inch until I engage levers A and B."

Just then my friend Retch Sweeney showed up. "What's that contraption?"

"A sod-cutter. I have to cut some sod."

"I thought we were going fishing."

"We are. That's why I have this machine. It will zip out the sod in no time, and then we can go fishing."

"The sod can wait. It ain't goin' nowhere, if I know sod. We'll miss the evening feed while you're foolin' around with sod."

"Be done in a couple of minutes," I said. That's when I heard a horn honking. It was Jake Stuff speeding down the street toward us in his pickup truck. I waved a greeting at him and jerked the pull-cord. The engine thundered to life on the first stroke, an event never before experienced by mankind in its long and frustrating relationship with rental machines.

Afterwards, Retch drove me down to the emergency room to get my hand checked out and bandaged.

"Looks to me like you bunged up your casting hand," he said. "Maybe you should have the doctor bandage a fly rod right to your hand. No tellin' how long it will take to heal up."

"Good idea," I said. "I don't know exactly what happened. My best guess is that I got my hand wedged between the sod-cutter handle and the fence—or maybe it was the side of Finley's house."

"Didn't cut much sod, as far as I could see," Retch said. "Those two big old steel teeth just kept chomping up the grass. I expect it goes a lot slower when it's actually cutting sod."

"I suppose," I said. "I must have engaged the wrong levers."

"Didn't hurt the fence all that much. Took out a couple boards is all, right about where Finley was standing. Old Finley's got some pretty good moves, don't he?"

"I thought so. Otherwise, the sod-cutter would have had

him a couple of times, once when we crossed his patio and the other time when he climbed that tree in the McFarlands' yard. Odd how that sod-cutter stayed right on his heels, like it had a mind of its own."

"Yeah," Retch said. "Finley probably thinks you were chasing him with it. I know that's what I thought."

"I'm sure he does. Still, I considered it rather rude, the way he kept shouting for someone to call the SWAT team."

While I was getting my hand bandaged in the emergency room, Finley was wheeled past the door in a wheelchair. I raised a hand to him in greeting. He gestured back. The longer I know him, the more irritable Finley becomes. Probably just part of the aging process. It turned out he was suffering from nothing more than a little overexertion and stress, and they don't award bandages for overexertion and stress. Served Finley right.

I must say the guys down at Kelly's were totally enthralled by my report on how I had come to have a bandage on my hand. Indeed, scarcely had I ended my story than Mel turned to Stumpy and exclaimed, "What did you catch 'em on, flies or worms?"

Thusly does a simple bandage on a person's hand hold endless fascination for men who do real work.

As for the sod-cutter, no one seems to know the reason for its erratic behavior. From my own understanding of machines, however, I would have to say that it was probably possessed by evil spirits. But that's only an educated guess.

The Big Woods

CRAZY EDDIE MULDOON and I had hit a dead spot in an otherwise interesting summer, mostly because Eddie's parents had confined him to his own yard for two weeks. This was shortly after Eddie's father, Mr. Muldoon, had fallen into a pit we had dug for the purpose of trapping wild animals, which we intended to tame and then train to do tricks. Eddie had even found an old chair and made a whip out of a stick and a length of clothesline. Those were the main things you needed to train wild animals, a chair and a whip. Eddie planned to charge people to see the animals perform. It was a good idea and probably would have made Eddie and me some money, but then Eddie's father fell in the pit and ruined everything. Mr. Muldoon wasn't hurt one bit, and neither was the skunk, the only wild animal in the trap at the time, not counting Mr. Muldoon. From all the fuss, a person would have thought we had dug the trap just for Eddie's father. It was the wild-

animal trap that got Eddie confined to his yard. After the
first week, I was allowed in to play with him, and it was a
good thing, too. Eddie was about ready to go yard-crazy.

"How's it going?" I asked.

"Terrible," he said. "The guards are real mean to me,
particularly the one that smells like skunk."

"What do they feed you?"

"Just bread and water. But I've set some snares around
the yard to see if I can catch something for supper. Look, a
wild pig!" He pointed to a Muldoon chicken approaching one
of his snares. The chicken stepped into the snare and pecked
at some crumbs Eddie had left on the ground, then wandered
off without tripping the snare. Eddie was furious. He took
great pride in his snares, even though he had never caught
anything with one of them. "Stupid chicken!" he yelled.

About then one of the guards appeared at the door and
said lunch was ready. Eddie and I went in. The guard had
placed bowls of soup and a platter of ham sandwiches and a
pitcher of lemonade on the table. "Usually, it's just bread
and water," Eddie explained as we washed our hands. "The
guard didn't want the outside world to know how mean they
are to me."

"Go tell your father lunch is ready," the guard said to
Eddie.

Eddie sniffed the air. "He's coming now."

And at that moment Mr. Muldoon stepped on the porch
and opened the screen door. He looked at me. "Aha, the
other wild-animal tamer," he growled.

"Now, Herbert," Mrs. Muldoon said. "Don't get all
fussed up again. The boys just let their imaginations run
away from them from time to time."

"Only kidding," Mr. Muldoon said. "But it wouldn't

hurt if they penned up their imaginations for the rest of the summer. Eddie must get his imagination from your side of the family. I've never imagined anything in my life. Boys have got to learn to live in the real world. Take life like it is, and no complaints. You ever hear me complain? Never!"

"That's good, Herbert, because I have a little job for you. I need some dewberries for jam, and I want you to take the boys out in the woods and pick me a couple of gallons."

Mr. Muldoon started to complain.

"Hooray!" Eddie and I shouted in unison. "You mean the Big Woods, Ma?" Eddie cried.

Mr. Muldoon went on complaining.

"Yes, dear, the Big Woods."

Mr. Muldoon complained even more fiercely. It was hard to believe this was his first time, he did it so well.

"Great!" Eddie yelled. "Maybe we'll even get lost out in the Big Woods and have to build snares to survive. Pat and I will go get the berry buckets out of the garage."

As soon as Mr. Muldoon had finished his lunch, Eddie and I raced across the highway toward the Big Woods, with Mr. Muldoon plodding along behind. Mrs. Muldoon stood in the doorway and watched our departure. "You keep a close eye on the boys, Herbert," she called after us. "It would be easy for them to wander off and get lost."

Mr. Muldoon chortled evilly.

Eddie and I had named the Big Woods ourselves. There were lots of little woods around that we were allowed to play in, but the Big Woods went on forever. They spread out across the valley, over the foothills, and then climbed the mountains. I was a little concerned about getting lost in the Big Woods, because I didn't have that much faith in Eddie's snares as a means of providing sustenance.

Eddie and I raced along a trail overgrown with ferns taller than ourselves. "Hold up, you rascals!" Mr. Muldoon shouted. "I ain't wearing tennis shoes, like you. Even if a bear was chasin' me, all I could do is walk a little faster." Eddie's father actually grinned at us. He seemed to be enjoying the hike through the woods, even in his big old clodhopper boots. They probably weighed five pounds each.

Eddie and I enjoyed the hike, too. The woods were cool and moist and full of a thousand shades of green, with thick blankets of moss covering long-dead fallen trees. Shafts of sunlight slanted through the towering firs and pines and cedars, making bright green blotches in the shadowy woods. Out there in the shadows, perhaps even watching us, were deer and elk and cougars and bears and—!

"Bear!" screamed Crazy Eddie. He pointed into the woods. And there it was! Eight feet tall, mean red eyes glaring from its black hairy head, the fanged mouth twisted back in a horrible snarl!

For a brief moment, Mr. Muldoon seemed almost as startled as I. "That's only a black stump, Eddie," he explained crossly. He picked his hat up off the trail and put it back on his head. "What did I tell you about that imagination of yours! Stop letting it run wild!"

I couldn't believe Eddie had actually mistaken the stump for a bear, and told him so. Anyone could see it was just a stupid old black stump.

The woods became less enjoyable after our encounter with the stump. "It could have been a bear," Eddie said. Both he and I now looked for other signs of bear in the shadows. We dropped back and followed close behind Mr. Muldoon, who from time to time turned his head casually to peer off to the left and then to the right, probably to check for landmarks. The woods had grown darker and were full of rustling and cracking and creaking sounds we hadn't noticed before.

"How come your mom just doesn't make raspberry jam?" I said to Eddie. "Raspberry jam is good."

"I don't know," Eddie said nervously. "I think raspberry jam would be plenty good enough, don't you, Pa?"

"We come to pick dewberries and we are going to pick dewberries," Mr. Muldoon grumbled. "Bears or no bears."

A few minutes later, the woods thinned and faded away tree by tree, and all at once we were in a big bright clearing, larger than the Muldoons' cow pasture. Dewberry vines were everywhere, climbing over ancient brush piles and gray stumps, the vines heavy with black juicy fruit.

"Wow!" Crazy Eddie said. "Look at all the dewberries! Did you know this clearing was here, Pa?"

"Of course I knew it was here," Mr. Muldoon said, smiling. "Did you think I was leading you on a wild-goose chase?"

We went to picking dewberries with a frenzy, stopping only occasionally to gobble handfuls of the sweet, juicy fruit. Eddie and I both exchanged the opinion that dewberries made much better jam than raspberry. As we exhausted each trove of berries, we moved deeper into the clearing, our buckets growing ever heavier. Then Eddie and I spotted a pile of stones black with berries. We raced each other to get to it first. The pile of stones turned out to be the remains of a fireplace. Hidden beneath the grass was the stone foundation of a cabin.

Some distance off were the remains of another fireplace. And beyond that another. And still another. Gray, weathered boards and cedar shakes were scattered about on the ground. Near one of the cabin sites was a patch of wild roses and a gnarled fruit tree.

"Hey, Pa," Eddie called out. "Somebody used to live here. This was once a little town."

Mr. Muldoon straightened up from a tangle of berry vines and rubbed his back. "Yeah," he said. "A long time ago. You guys got your buckets full yet?"

"Just about," Eddie said.

The sun slid down behind the great dark mass of the Big Woods. A cool breeze stirred the tall dry grass of the clearing.

Mr. Muldoon walked over to look at the fireplace.

"What do you suppose happened to the people who lived here?" Eddie asked him.

"Oh, they probably moved away," Mr. Muldoon said.

"Why would they do that?" Eddie said.

"How should I know?" Mr. Muldoon said.

A lone raven flew over, silent except for the rustle of its wings.

"Maybe they were all murdered," Eddie said. "Some bandits came along and murdered them."

"They weren't murdered," Mr. Muldoon said. "They moved away."

A board clattered to the ground on the far side of the clearing. We stared in the direction of the sound. Nothing there. The breeze sighed through the tall grass, as though whispering to us of some dreadful mystery of long ago.

"The murdered people are probably buried under those roses," Eddie said. I looked at the patch of wild roses. It seemed likely. Otherwise, what would wild roses be doing out in the middle of a clearing?

"There are probably ghosts here, don't you think, Pa?" Eddie said. "The ghosts of the poor murdered people."

"Eddie," Mr. Muldoon said. "There's no such thing as

ghosts. There you go again, letting your imagination—what's that?"

"What's what, Pa?"

"Nothing. Just the wind I guess."

"Could have been a ghost," Eddie said. "What did it sound like, Pa?"

Mr. Muldoon didn't reply. He seemed absorbed in thought, possibly reassessing his opinion about the existence of ghosts.

"Gosh," I said. "Maybe I'd better be heading home."

"Me too," Eddie said. "It's probably about the time the ghosts come out. I bet they wander around the clearing out here talking to each other after dark, just like they did before they were murdered."

"Eddie. . . ." Mr. Muldoon said, stroking the hair on the back of his neck.

A rock tumbled from the fireplace chimney. All three of us jumped. Mr. Muldoon picked his hat up off the ground and slapped it back on his head.

"Yeah," I said. "I'd better head on home." I turned and sauntered toward the entrance of the trail through the Big Woods. I could hear the grass whispering all around me. I sauntered faster. Eddie passed me at a quick walk. I started to trot to keep up. Eddie broke into a run. I ran past him. Eddie passed me. I had the distinct feeling something was after us. Now Eddie and I were flying down the trail, running harder and harder, cold sweat streaming out behind. I could hear things gaining on us, an eerie angry rumbling coming closer and closer. We sailed over logs across the trail without even touching them, logs so big Mr. Muldoon had to boost us over them on the way into the dreadful clearing. Eddie slipped and fell, and I leaped over him without even breaking stride and kept going. It was each man for himself now. Eddie shot past me a second later. And at last we burst out of the woods and slid to a stop in the ditch by the highway. The drivers of the cars going by glanced out at us, little realizing they were looking at two boys who had just made a desperate escape from an unknown number of irate ghosts.

"I sure hope the ghosts didn't get Pa," Eddie gasped.

"Me too," I said.

"Whewee!" Mr. Muldoon said.

Eddie and I whirled around. We thought he'd still be back in the clearing. I couldn't help but stare down at his big old clodhopper boots, to make sure he was still wearing them. He was. They seemed to be giving off steam, but that may have just been my imagination.

Mr. Muldoon sucked in a draft of air, as he glanced back up the trail behind us. "Well, that was invigorating. *Gasp!* So, you boys thought you could—*gasp*—race the old man home, did you? Wheweee! I guess I showed you I could—*choke*—hold my own with a couple of kids, even after a late start."

We crossed the highway into Eddie's yard, with Mr. Muldoon stopping to rest every few feet. He seemed a little shaky. "Yep, that was—*gasp*—quite a race," he said. "I probably would have beaten the two of you, if I hadn't been worried about spilling my bucket of berries. Look here—*gasp*—I didn't lose a single ber—!"

And then Mr. Muldoon slammed facedown on the ground, sending the berries spraying from his bucket.

"Pa!" Eddie cried out. "Are you all right? What's the matter, Pa? Your heart? Is it your heart?"

Eddie's father rolled over on his back and propped himself up on his elbows. All three of us looked down at his foot. One of Eddie's snares had finally caught something.

Elk Magic

AFTER MANY YEARS of hard work, I have managed to create a reputation for myself of not catching fish and not shooting game. I don't mean to brag, but I have been in situations where a twelve-year-old boy with a slingshot could have limited out, and I have still managed to come away empty-handed. My psychologist friend Paul Quinnett a few years ago wrote an article in which he testified as an expert witness to my rare ability not only to catch no fish but to prevent anyone within a radius of a hundred yards from catching fish. Indeed, such is my reputation around town that people here won't even think about going fishing or hunting on a day when they know I'm abroad with rod or gun anywhere in the state. It's a special talent.

Some of the best guides and outfitters in the country have bragged that they were so good there was no way I could come back from an excursion with them without bagging fish or game. I have accepted numerous of these challenges and have yet to be defeated. Sadly, I heard later that many of these guides and outfitters afterwards took to drink. Others lost all faith in their skills and wound up among the homeless, stumbling along the streets of large cities and mumbling absurdities like, "I know the elk were there, but McManus, he did something, radiated out some kind of magnetic field or . . ." One outfitter even sold his pack string, went to law school, and became a successful attorney. How would you like that on your conscience?

I must admit that I'd become pretty smug about never catching fish or shooting game. Sure, I was even a bit cocky, maybe even too cocky, that day I was sitting in a hotel lounge in Denver when a shadow fell across my table. I looked up into the smiling face of Paul Howard, the former offensive lineman for the Denver Broncos. Paul now owned Proline Excursions out of Denver.

We chatted for a while, and then Paul said, "I've got a proposition for you, Pat. You come hunt with me, and I'll guarantee you an elk."

I laughed and shook my head. "No way, Paul. You're too nice a guy. I've ruined too many outfitters who thought they could go up against my reputation, and I've beaten them all. You hunt with me, you could end up as a . . . a . . . an attorney."

Paul shuddered at the thought, and a tiny doubt flickered in his eyes for a split second. That is one of the things you watch for when an outfitter tries to call you out. It gives you an edge, and sometimes that's all you need.

"I know your reputation," Paul said. "And I know the risks. But I've got a place where even you cannot help but get an elk. We had a hundred percent success rate on our last hunt. Most of these guys had never even seen an elk before, let alone shot one."

I had heard it all before. Hunters kept awake all night by elk bugling around their camp. Traffic on the roads held up for hours by streams of elk passing through. Hunters who wouldn't pull the trigger on bulls with racks the size of forklifts, because they thought they were dreaming. And so on.

Paul's challenge was mighty tempting, though. These days, I was about as popular with outfitters as sushi at a cattlemen's barbecue. It had been years since I added another notch to my rifle stock, which was already pretty well eaten away from notches recording the other outfitters I had defeated. From the way Paul described his ranch, I knew this would be a major challenge, and a major notch. I only hoped there was enough wood left in the stock to take it.

"Okay, Paul," I said, "you're on. I'll meet you at the crack of dawn one year from today."

"Great!"

"One question."

"Sure."

"What time does dawn crack around here?"

Paul told me.

"In that case, we'll meet two hours after the crack of dawn."

As the year passed, I became increasingly uneasy about my hunt with Paul Howard. He was and still is a great athlete. Maybe he would expect me to keep up with him as he charged up and down the mountains of Colorado, which start where other mountains end and go up from there—way up. In order to survive such a hunt, I would have to spend the next six months running five miles a day, lifting weights, dieting. I called up Paul and told him a life-and-death situation had come up, and I wouldn't be able to hunt with him after all.

"I can drive you right up to the hunting area," Paul said, "and you just sit there until an elk you like comes by."

"Really? Hold on a second, Paul, my secretary just handed me a note. Hey, this is wonderful! The life-and-death situation has just been canceled."

"What a coincidence!"

Little did Paul realize I hadn't been handed a note at all. I don't even have a secretary! These outfitters are so easy to fool.

I should mention here that the stakes in these challenges are high for me, too. I make my living by writing about being unsuccessful in outdoor sports. If I go on an outing and have a good time, it's ruined for me. If everything goes wrong, I'm delighted. Once, my friends Gary Roedl and Keith Jackson and I were stranded by a stalled pickup truck at the bottom of a remote canyon in Montana in the middle of a blizzard. The situation was desperate. Roedl and Jackson looked grim. I burst out laughing. "Bad enough we're all going to freeze to death," Jackson said, "but we have to put up with a crazy person while we do it."

Unsuccess is my meat and potatoes. If I were a successful and expert hunter, I could be Jim Zumbo, and Jim Zumbo could be me. As a matter of fact, I have suggested several times that we exchange identities. Zumbo always says, "Let me think about it. Naw."

But now Paul Howard had presented me with a formidable challenge. If he managed to put an elk within the range of my marksmanship, which is close, he would win, whether or not I shot the elk. That's the way the game is played. I had plenty to lose. A whole career of unsuccess could be wiped out in a single moment by one stupid elk.

The day of the elk hunt finally arrived. Kathy Howard, Paul's wife, picked me up at the airport. Kathy is a funny and very classy person, but she didn't ease my concern about the hunt. "I'm so sick of elk!" she confessed. "Elk elk elk elk! That's all anyone talks about up at the ranch. Who got the biggest rack. Who made the best shot. Every hunter who shows up thinks his elk is the greatest."

"Every hunter?" I said. "Every hunter has got an elk?"

"So far this year. It's all just so boring! Well, we have a new group in now. Maybe they'll be able to talk about something besides elk."

"I doubt it," I said. I know elk hunters.

As we approached the ranch, Kathy suddenly braked.

"What is it?" I asked.

"Elk," she said.

And it was true. A herd of elk bounded down the bank just ahead of us and streamed across the road. I couldn't believe it, and I don't expect anyone else to, but it happened. I was immediately overcome with a terrible sense of foreboding.

"Elk elk elk," Kathy said. "I can't even drive to town without practically getting run over by elk."

"It's terrible," I said. I meant it, too.

We had a magnificent feed at the Winslett Ranch that night. The Howards, ranchowners Allan and Jeanne Jones, and I thoroughly enjoyed it. But all the other newly arrived hunters were so joyous with expectation they could barely eat. They had come from all parts of the United States, seeking that fabled "hunt of a lifetime." A pleasant chap by the name of Russ came all the way from Long Island. This was his first elk hunt. He was so beside himself with excitement that I didn't know which of him to talk to.

That night I bunked in a cozy and picturesque log cabin that had once been the ranch's one-room schoolhouse. I was thoroughly comfortable, but I had trouble getting to sleep, what with all the elk bugling outside. The ranch definitely needed a curfew, with all the elk to be shut off at 10 P.M.

Forgetting what I had told him a year earlier, Paul woke us up well before the crack of dawn, herded us into the ranch house and stuffed us with a gargantuan breakfast. Afterwards, he loaded Russ and me into a 4×4 pickup truck, and we clawed our way farther up into the mountains. Some of the grades were mere precipices but there were steep places, too. On several occasions, both Russ and I were beside ourselves with excitement, which made for a pretty crowded pickup cab.

Finally reaching a plateau of sorts, Paul parked the truck and we got out, softly closing the doors so as not to disturb the elk. I was jittery. It looked as though in a few moments I would have to shoot an elk. Paul placed Russ and me on stands. Shortly thereafter a sliver of sun appeared on the horizon. It was the first time I had ever seen the sun rise from below me. Colorado mountains are high.

"Get ready," Paul whispered to me. "Some elk should be coming by any minute now. And remember, don't take the first big bull you see. Wait for a nice one."

"Right," I said. Sweat trickled down my back. I stared at the freshly churned-up ground where a herd of elk had recently passed not more than twenty-five yards in front of me.

It would be an easy shot. I hate easy shots. They don't allow you any excuse for missing.

The sun rose higher in the sky. "They should be here by now," Paul said. He looked around, a puzzled expression on his face. "They've been moving through here every morning. I scouted it out just for you."

My old confidence began to return. I smiled.

"They're probably bedded in those aspens down there," Paul said nervously. "I'll make a sweep around the bottom of the ridge and drive them up past you and Russ. Remember, pick out a good one."

"Sure," I said. Paul headed for the grove of aspens. Off in the distance I could see Russ on his stand, rifle at the ready, his posture tense with expectation. I removed my hunting jacket and sat down on it. Then I poured myself a cup of coffee. I thought about taking a nap. I recognized the situation: The outfitter turning panicky. The outfitter rushing off to drive elk toward me. I laughed, without fear of being heard by elk.

An hour later, Paul came puffing up the steep slope. "See anything?"

"Nothing."

"I don't know what's wrong," Paul said, wiping his face with a kerchief. This place is always crawling with elk. Well, if they aren't here, I know where they'll be."

We piled into the pickup and drove to another place. The elk weren't there either. Paul was dumbfounded. He had never before come up against my kind of magic.

Driving out in the dark that night, we passed a deep, heavily forested canyon. We could hear the elk down there, bugling like mad.

"So that's where they went to," Paul said. "That's really odd. I've never known elk to hole up in that particular canyon before. Well, at least we know where they are. We'll get 'em tomorrow."

I stifled a laugh. I knew what the elk were doing down in that canyon. They were making travel plans. The leader of the herd was drawing maps in the dirt with a hoof. "Okay, gang," he was saying, "we had a close call today, because we didn't know Pat was coming on the hunt. Fortunately, we were able to hide out in this canyon we've never hidden out in before. Now's our chance to clear out. Here we have Hawaii and here we have the Northwest Territories. Hawaii is a long swim, so we'd better head for the Northwest Territories. We owe it to Pat. Mount up! Yo!"

The next morning the elk were gone from the canyon. That evening reports began to come in from other hunters who hadn't seen an elk for dozens of miles in any direction. Paul's other hunters stared grimly at him over supper that night. Russ was so disappointed he could hardly talk. I liked Russ a lot, and Paul, too, and I knew what I had to do. I took Paul aside.

"I'm pulling out of here first thing in the morning," I told him. "I just can't do this to all these good folks. Going soft I guess."

"Gee, I really appreciate that, Pat," Paul said. "I thought I could beat you, but I see now that's not possible. You're the best I've ever seen."

"Thanks," I said. "I'll be out of the state by tomorrow night. The elk can't be more than a day's trek away. They'll come flooding back in as soon as I'm gone."

As it happened, the elk didn't even wait until I was out

of the state. As Kathy was driving me off the ranch on my way back to Denver, she slammed on the brakes. A herd of elk streamed across the road ahead of us.

"Elk elk elk!" she yelled in exasperation.

I heard later that Russ got a seven-point bull that very day. I guess he must have taken the first one that came along, but beginning elk hunters tend to do that.

As Kathy and I sat in the car waiting for the elk to pass, I unsheathed my rifle. "What are you doing with your rifle?" Kathy asked. "You can't shoot from the road."

"I'm just carving a notch in the stock," I said. "A big notch."

"But you didn't get an elk!"

I guess Kathy hadn't heard about my reputation.

There She Blows

I'VE NEVER HAD any luck with collecting as a hobby. When I think of all the cheap and useless things I could have collected over the years that are now worth a fortune, it makes me sick. I read a while back about an old duck decoy selling for thousands of dollars. It didn't look like much either. I recently whittled a brand-new duck decoy that looked twice as good as that old one, and it isn't worth more than a piece of firewood. That's because it isn't old, won't be for at least another fifty years or so, and I lack the patience to wait that long. The older something is, the more it is valued, people being the only exception. The older people get the more they go down in value. If you don't believe me, just put a weathered old wooden duck decoy and a weathered old man up for auction and see who gets the highest bid. I can tell you right now it will be the duck. It's not because collectors don't like old men, but because they know value when they see it. Fool that I am, I started out early in life collecting old men, and I got a lot of use out of them, too, mostly in the form of entertainment, but every last one of them depreciated down to nothing. I guess I just lacked good business sense.

My friend Crazy Eddie Muldoon and I got bitten by the collecting bug, and by quite a few other bugs, too, when we were about ten years old. We knew lots of kids who were already well started on collecting, mostly dumb stuff like comic books and baseball cards that any fool could see would never be worth more than the paper they were printed on, but of course you can't expect kids to have any business sense. Oliver Smith, a rich kid who lived in town, collected model steam engines—working steam engines! There was something worth collecting. Oliver knew what he was doing. Every birthday he got a new toy steam engine that actually got up a head of steam that sent its little flywheel spinning. Because of our religious upbringing, Eddie and I certainly wouldn't have killed for one measly steam engine. Serious maiming, however, would not have been out of the question. We were returning from one of Oliver's birthday parties, stuffed with cake and ice cream and envy, when Eddie came up with a fantastic idea.

"I think we should collect steam engines," he said.

"Me too," I said. "Our folks will buy us steam engines as soon as chickens learn to tap dance. I can hardly wait."

"Of course they're not going to buy us steam engines," Eddie said. "We'll have to build them."

"You know how to build steam engines?"

"Sure. There's not much to them. Come on over to the house tomorrow and we'll build one."

Eddie's enthusiasm for his various inventions was highly

contagious, and I soon had a bad case of it myself, with good reason. After all, Eddie and I had built and tested a submarine, deep-sea diving gear, a live trap for wild animals, and an airplane we piloted off a barn roof. In every instance we had survived. Surely, we could build a simple little steam engine with which to start our collection.

We set to work on the steam engine early the next morning, using the Muldoon cellar as our workshop. Eddie had gathered together a large old tin fly sprayer, a metal wheel off a garden cultivator, a bunch of candles, a wooden box, baling wire, a metal curtain rod, a pie pan, nails, and various other materials. I could see right away that his plan emphasized function over design. Somehow, I had imagined a little gleaming brass engine, but that could come later. First we needed to build the prototype.

"Here's the idea," Eddie said. "We build a frame to hold the fly sprayer up above the box. We attach the curtain rod to the handle of the sprayer and run it to the cultivator wheel. Then we fill the reservoir of the sprayer with water. Next we put the candles in the pie pan under the reservoir and light them. A head of steam will build up in the reservoir and push the plunger on the handle back out, which will turn the flywheel. I have already drilled a hole in the tube around the plunger. When the plunger goes past that hole, the steam will be released, the flywheel will turn and shove the plunger back, and then the steam will shove it back again, and away it will go, *chug chug chug!*"

"Sounds good to me," I said.

By the time Mrs. Muldoon called Eddie and me up for lunch, the steam engine was built and ready for testing. It was only with great effort that we could contain our excitement as we sat down to soup and sandwiches with Eddie's parents and Mr. and Mrs. Haverstead, who had come to buy some hay and been invited to stay for lunch.

"What have you boys been up to?" Mrs. Haverstead asked, perhaps not entirely out of curiosity, for Eddie and I had acquired considerable notoriety as a result of our inventions.

"We're working on an invention," Eddie said.

"How nice, dear," Mrs. Haverstead said.

"Just so it's not another airplane on the barn roof," Mr. Muldoon grumbled. One whole side of his face twitched. I had noticed that every time Mr. Muldoon mentioned our airplane, which he did often, his face twitched like that. You would have thought he had been in the airplane with Eddie and me when it soared off the barn roof. Now there was something to make a face twitch!

"Or a deep-sea diving helmet," Mrs. Muldoon said. That caused Mr. Muldoon's face to twitch again.

"Well, think of it this way, Herb," Mr. Haverstead said to Mr. Muldoon. "Maybe the boys will turn out to be great engineers when they grow up—if they do! Ha ha!"

"Ha ha," Mr. Muldoon said.

As soon as lunch was over, Eddie and I rushed back down to the cellar to test the steam engine, leaving Eddie's parents and the Haversteads visiting over coffee.

"Let's hurry and get the steam engine running," Eddie said. "I want Mr. Haverstead to see it. Did you hear him say how we might become great engineers?"

"Yeah."

Eddie took out a kitchen match and lit the candles arranged under the reservoir of the fly sprayer—I mean under the boiler of the steam engine.

We stood back and watched the bottom of the boiler blacken with candle smoke. This being a very basic steam engine, it lacked any gauges to indicate when sufficient pressure had built up in the boiler to push the drive rod and send the flywheel spinning. We watched the boiler grow blacker and blacker. We watched the drive rod begin to tremble. We watched the whole steam engine begin to shake. But the stupid drive rod refused to move! Not a single *chug* emanated from the engine! Eddie and I looked at each other. Eddie smiled, nervously wiping a bead of sweat off his upper lip. The cellar seemed to be heating up. Then, popping tinnily, the ends of the boiler bulged out! The two engineers leaped back. Instead of *chug chug,* the engine was making an ominous ticking sound, perhaps not unlike a time bomb.

"It's going to blow!" Eddie yelped, a prediction I had arrived at on my own but not soon enough to beat my colleague to the cellar stairs. We burst into the kitchen, our hands clasped over our ears, always mindful to protect our hearing from loud noises, and raced toward the nearest exit. The Muldoons and the Haversteads glanced at us with considerable interest. Mr. Haverstead was apparently in the middle of a fishing story, because I caught the words "had just cast next to this log when—"

"It's going to blow!" shouted Eddie.

This announcement not only had a most stimulating effect on the four adults but seemed to seize them bodily and jerk them out of their chairs, one of which flew across the kitchen and ricocheted off the stove. A mere second later, the six of us were standing in the yard, staring back at the house, the ladies with their hands clasped over their ears.

"What is it, a bomb?" shouted Mr. Muldoon at Eddie. "How big a bomb is it?"

"—a monster bass hit," said Mr. Haverstead, who was still holding his coffee cup.

"It's a steam engine," Eddie said. "It was just getting up a head of steam and we . . ."

Faintly, from inside the house, came a sound—*phimpp!*

"What was that?" said Mr. Muldoon.

"The boiler," Eddie said. "The boiler just blew up. I was expecting something bigger."

One whole side of Mr. Muldoon's face twitched.

After Mr. Muldoon got done ranting and raving and throwing in a mild cussword here and there for punctuation, the little crowd of us trooped down the basement to survey the damage. There wasn't much damage. Through a rapidly dissipating cloud of steam, we could make out the little engine that couldn't. Water from the boiler had extinguished the candles and puddled out onto the floor. It was a pretty depressing sight.

"My fly sprayer!" croaked Mr. Muldoon.

"Now now, dear, you haven't used it in years," Mrs. Muldoon said.

"Got to encourage the boys, Herb," Mr. Haverstead said. "They may grow up to be great engineers. Just because their steam engine didn't work, doesn't mean they won't."

"Good gosh!" Eddie suddenly exclaimed, bending over to look at the remains of the engine. "It worked! It worked!"

And sure enough, it had. The drive shaft had been pushed out and turned the flywheel, half a turn anyway. But Eddie and I hadn't been there to see this miracle of technology, or to hear what surely must have been a single mighty *CHUG!*

Still, I couldn't help but smile. It wasn't often our inventions worked so well. The Haversteads and Mrs. Muldoon smiled, too. After a bit, even Mr. Muldoon smiled slightly, and if I hadn't been watching his face so closely, I probably wouldn't even have noticed the tiny twitch.

Brimstone

GOD CREATED MARCH in case eternity should prove too brief." I penned that line many years ago, back in the days when I still harbored literary pretensions, and I am pleased to see that it has stood the test of time. In all modesty, I think it's rather Shakespearian. It also remains an accurate description of March, the longest month by far, something more than a thousand days by my reckoning.

March may be somewhat shorter in southern states, but here in the North it stretches on forever, wet and cold and full of wind and slush. Hunting is long past, fishing yet to come, and camping but a dream. I stand at the window and stare vacantly out into the blustery gloom, a chinook devouring banks of gray, grubby snow, water streaming down the road and pooling in the yard, wind lashing the dark, leafless trees, the air filled with an incessant whine.

"Will you stop that incessant whining!" my wife, Bun,

yells at me. "All you do day after day is stand at that window and stare vacantly into space. Why don't you get a hobby of some kind?"

"Staring vacantly into space is my hobby," I respond sharply. "My March hobby. I loathe March."

"Poor baby."

One thing I hate even worse than March is mock sympathy from a smart-alecky spouse. Bun is a master of the form.

It being evident that I can expect no sympathy from my wife of many Marches, I continue to stare vacantly out the window, trying to console myself with the fact that this is by no means the longest March I have ever experienced. The longest March occurred back when I was about fifteen, or at least somewhere around the middle of those horrible teenage years when the world is your oyster, but you can't pry it open.

March came early that year to our little town of Blight, Idaho, and stayed late. In other parts of the world, it was probably April or May or even June, but in Blight it was still ugly old March, the season of mud. We woke up with mud, went to bed with mud, and dreamed fitfully of mud. The thaw had come. We had spent the entire winter shoveling snow, but it did no good to shovel mud. Mud just goes down forever. If your car got stuck in a mud hole, and you started shoveling it out, pretty soon your car would be stuck in a well. It was not unusual to be driving in that distant and gentler time and actually stop when a stranger on the road flagged you down.

"I got my car stuck in the mud," he'd say. "Could you tow it out for me?"

"Sure," you'd reply. "Where's your car?"

"I'm standing on it."

Right then you would know that here was a man who had tried to shovel his car out of the mud.

When your car got stuck in the mud, any car trying to tow you out would also probably get stuck in the mud. So what you did was to go find a man with a horse, a big strong horse, one that could tow your car out of the mud. It was that very chore, finding a tow horse, that was thrust upon me so many miserable Marches ago.

All week I had been incarcerated in Delmore Blight High School, where, among other unmentionable atrocities, I was daily exposed to the corpse of Latin, a language that had been dead so long it was almost unrecognizable. If Latin hadn't already been dead, I personally would have been only too happy to kill it. Then the weekend arrived, but a weekend filled with nothing but ugly March. Mud. Rain. Sleet. Wind. The whole world seemingly had filled up with icy swirling mud-brown water. All Saturday morning I stood at the window staring vacantly out. March stared back, grinning fiendishly.

"Don't just stand there staring vacantly out into space," my mother scolded. "For heaven's sake, find yourself a hobby!"

"Staring vacantly into space is my hobby."

It's always good to get an early start on your hobbies.

As I stood there staring vacantly into space, my eyes suddenly focused on a sheriff's car plowing in through the mud of our farm road. Hastily reviewing my activities of the previous week, I relaxed, confident that the visit from the law had nothing to do with me.

"Hey, Ma," I yelled. "Guess who's coming in? Deputy Wiley Dipp."

"That miserable little twerp! I wonder what he wants. If

you shot off another sewer-pipe cannon down at the golf course, you're in for it."

"Look, Ma, eyebrows. I'm done fooling with black powder. I like eyebrows. I like skin."

"That's nice. Now go answer the door."

I let Wiley stand outside in the rain a few moments, water streaming off the brim of his cowboy hat as he glowered at me. The deputy was one of my least favorite people. "Which of the womenfolk did you come for, Wiley?" I asked, opening the door.

"Don't smart-mouth me, kid. Where's your mom?"

"Here she comes now. What's up?"

"Rancid Crabtree is what's up. I'm going to arrest him."

"Arrest Rancid?" Mom and I gasped in unison.

Rancid Crabtree was a kindly old woodsman who lived in a little shack back against the mountain, a gentle soul who never bothered anybody. He was also my much-beloved mentor, teaching me all about woodsmanship and lots of other stuff, some of which I was pretty sure my mother didn't want me to know. Rancid was a serious student of hygiene. Long ago he figured out that it was unwise ever to take baths, because they eat holes in your protective crust and allow germs to get at you. My mother didn't agree with Rancid's theory, however, and I was forced to take at least one bath a week and thus catch colds. Mom's own theory about why Rancid never caught colds was that the germs couldn't stomach the smell and left him alone.

"Yep," Wiley said, "Crabtree deliberately broke a pool cue down at Bart's Saloon Saturday night."

"That doesn't sound like a crime to me," Mom said.

"He broke it over Bart's head," Wiley said.

"That doesn't sound like a crime to me," Mom said.

"Then he threw Bart out the door of his own saloon."

"That doesn't sound like a crime to me," Mom said.

"The door was closed when Crabtree done it."

"Oh."

"Problem is," Wiley said, "I can't find Crabtree's shack so I can arrest him. I need the loan of the boy here to guide me out there."

I could barely restrain a laugh. Dumb ol' Wiley actually thought I'd show him how to find Rancid's shack, actually help him arrest my best friend in the whole world. Well, fat chance of that!

Sleet splattered so hard against the window of the deputy's car that we could barely see to make the turn from the highway onto the mud road that led back to Rancid's shack.

"Take another left up there," I told Wiley.

Odd that the deputy would still remember that unfortunate business with the sewer-pipe cannon. Apparently there was no statute of limitations on the crime of firing a croquet ball from a sewer pipe down a golf-course fairway. My friend Retch Sweeney and I had taken all the usual safety precautions, too, and had even called out "Fore!"

Wiley turned left. "You sure this is a road?" he whined. "It sure don't look like one."

"It's a road, Wiley," I said, hunched sullenly down into my mackinaw. "Pretty much of one anyway. Why do you ask?"

" 'Cause we're drivin' right toward a gol-durn lake, that's why!"

I yawned. "That's no lake."

"It ain't no lake? Well then, it's the biggest puddle I

ever seen. But I guess we can plow through it." Wiley tromped down on the gas pedal.

I'd never been to the ocean. So I had no idea how big waves got there, but I suspected the wave created by the impact of Wiley's car would have run a good second to the best the ocean had to offer. Steam billowed from under the hood, the lights went out, and the radio went dead.

"Holy bleep!" cried the deputy. "You're in for it now, boy! You told me this wasn't a lake!"

"It isn't a lake. It's a crick. See, the ice has jammed up down below and backed up the crick."

"Well, shoot, if it's a crick, there should be a bridge over it."

"There is a bridge over it. The bridge is just under a foot or so of water. Even though you couldn't see it, you landed the car smack on the bridge. I gotta hand it to you, Wiley, you're a pretty darn good driver."

Wiley ignored the compliment, and set about banging his forehead up and down on the steering wheel, as though that would get us out of the crick. It did no good at all, of course, except to improve my mood considerably. After a bit, Wiley said, "We got to find somebody with a horse to tow us out. You know anybody around here with a horse?"

"Only one person," I said.

"Who's that?"

"Rancid Crabtree."

Wiley carried on like a madman for a few moments, and then finally ordered me out of the car and into the crick, to go and fetch Rancid and his horse.

Having slogged half a mile through mud up to my knees, I was tired and miserable when I got to Rancid's shack. He invited me in, blew the dust out of his guest cup, and poured me a steaming jolt of black coffee. We chatted a while about the miseries of March, and how bored we were with everything, and how we couldn't wait for trout season to open and how we expected a better run than usual of cutthroat that spring.

I finished my cup of coffee and Rancid poured me another. He mentioned that he must have sprained his back, because it had been giving him a little trouble the past couple of days. "Probably jist all the wet and cold weather," he speculated. "Or maybe Ah lifted somethin' heavy and throwed it too hard. Anyway, what brang you out on a day like this?"

"Oh, I almost forgot. Wiley Dipp is coming to arrest you."

"He is? Hot dang! Thet's the best news Ah heard all March. Let's see, Ah'll take maw checkers and checkerboard, because Ah thank Murph is still in jail. Maw Tucker's still cookin' at the jail, ain't she? If ol' Wiley'd jist git the lead out, Ah could be thar in time fer supper. By the way, what's Wiley arrestin' me for?"

"Throwing Bart through the door without opening it first."

"Ah didn't know thet was a crime! If Ah'd know'd thet, Ah'd a done it the fust of March, 'stead of waitin' until dang near the middle."

"Glad you're so happy about paying your debt to society," I said. "But the problem is, Wiley's car is stuck in the crick and we have to harness old Brimstone to pull it out. Otherwise, you'll never make it to jail in time for supper."

"Wait jist a dang minute! Ah might as soon not go to jail as have to harness Brimstone! Oh, let's give it a try."

We went out to the little corral behind Rancid's shack, and Rancid and I and Brimstone went at it. Brimstone knocked me down and tried to stand on my head, but Rancid grabbed the horse around the neck and bit down on its ear and got his fingers twisted around the horse's lip, and then Brimstone tried to crush Rancid against a corral post. The old woodsman managed to escape, and Brimstone chased him around the corral a couple of times and finally cornered him, and then Rancid doubled up his fist and punched the horse squarely between the eyes, buckling its knees and stunning it long enough for us to get the bridle and harness in place.

"Shucks, thet was easier than Ah expected," Rancid said. "Now let's go pull the deputy's car out, so he kin arrest me and git me to jail in time fer supper."

When Rancid, Brimstone, and I arrived back at the deputy's car, Wiley was peering out through the rain-streaked windshield.

"C'mon out of thar and arrest me, Wiley," Rancid ordered. "I got to git to jail in time fer supper."

Wiley got out and waded through the swirling water. "I'll arrest you when I'm dang good and ready, Crabtree," he growled. "First thing, you got to tow my car back out of this lake."

"Fine with me," Rancid said. He drove Brimstone around to the back of the car. The horse seemed to be returning to its own ornery self, tentatively reaching around to take a bite out of Rancid's shoulder. The old woodsman pointed a cautionary finger at the horse, who then pretended merely to be admiring Rancid's mackinaw.

Wiley rubbed his jaw thoughtfully as he searched for a way to hook the tow chain to the vehicle. "I guess the only thing to do is for you to crawl under the car and hook the chain to the frame, Crabtree."

"Wahl, Ah don't thank thet's the only thang to do, Wiley. T'other thang to do if fer *you* to crawl under the car and hook the chain. Ah cain't hold maw breath thet long underwater. 'Sides thet, Ah strained maw back a couple days ago, and cain't do no strenuous exercise."

Wiley looked at me.

"Don't look at me, Wiley."

"I'm certainly not submerging myself under a foot of water to hook that chain," Wiley said. He looked at Brimstone. "I've got a better idea. I'll just commandeer your horse and ride back to a house that has a telephone and get some real help."

"But than you'll arrest me, right, Wiley, so Ah kin git to jail in time fer supper?"

"No, I ain't. I've decided jail's too good for you, Crabtree. You enjoy it too much. Go on back to your crummy shack."

"Gol-dang it, Wiley, here Ah come all the way out here in the rain and mud and now you won't arrest me. If thet don't rile me up somethin' fierce. And now yer stealin' maw horse. Ah shore hope you know how to set a horse, Wiley, 'cause if you don't, Old Joe here . . ."

"Old Joe?" I said.

"Yep, Old Joe," Rancid said.

Wiley laughed, tilting back his cowboy hat and dumping a quart of ice water down the back of his neck. "You call that nag a horse? Now give me a boost up."

Rancid and I plodded through the mud back to his cabin. "Wahl, shoot," Rancid said. "Ah had maw mouth all set fer some of Maw Tucker's cookin' at the jail. Durn thet

Wiley! But Ah'll tell you what. You stay fer supper and Ah'll fry us up some venison and gravy and biscuits."

"Sounds good to me," I said. "You think you'll ever get Brimstone back, Rance?"

"Oh, shore. Ah recollect the only time Ah tried to ride him. About five miles t'other side of the state line, he slowed down enough fer me to jump off. Thet offended Brimstone somethin' awful, and him and me went four rounds right on the spot, and Ah never come out ahead in a single one. Took me two days to walk back home. And thar was Brimstone, chompin' down hay in the corral. So don't you fret none about ol' Brimstone."

Three months later, March came to an end. And none too soon, either.

The Blue Dress

Rancid had warned us to be at his place at four o'clock sharp. "Iffen you're a minute late," he warned, "Ah'll leave with out yuhs!" Retch and I, both about twelve at the time, had chuckled to ourselves, because the rank old woodsman had about as much regard for time as he had for baths. So we came pumping our bikes up to his cabin a good hour after the crack of dawn. And Rancid's truck was gone.

"Can you beat that!" Retch said. "The ornery old codger left without us!"

"You can't trust anybody to keep an appointment anymore," I said. "Well, all we can do is ride our bikes up to the head of Sand Creek and see if we can find him before he's caught all the fish."

After five miles of pumping up the dirt road, we finally found Rancid's truck. We still didn't know whether he had fished upstream or downstream. If we couldn't find him, he might return to the truck while we were gone and take off, and we'd have to ride the bikes all the way back home.

We decided to start downstream and see if we could overtake him in that direction. As it happened, the fishing turned out to be so good that we soon forgot all about transportation one way or another, and didn't think of it again until well into the afternoon, when the sweltering heat began to drain our energy. The mere thought of having to pedal bikes all the way home suddenly became a matter of major concern.

"Geez, it's so hot, you know what I'd like to do?" Retch said. "I'd like to take off all my clothes and dive into a deep cool pool of that water."

"Me too," I said. "But we'd better find Rancid first."

We climbed up to the road and began trudging back toward Rancid's truck, our plodding feet making little explosions in the deep hot dust. By now we had figured out that Rancid had fished upstream, because our fishing wouldn't have been nearly so good if he had gone downstream. In those days Rancid usually considered a fishing limit to be all you could catch plus one fish. He would have left nothing for us.

Suddenly, we noticed a moving cloud of dust spewing into the air up ahead and thought for a moment it might be Rancid's truck. Then we saw it was a rusty old sedan and instantly realized to our horror that major trouble was headed our way—the infamous and evil Skragg boys!

The Skragg boys numbered approximately a dozen, ranging in age from eight to thirty or so, their degrees of meanness increasing gradually in magnitude from youngest to eldest, with the youngest possessing the least pleasing attributes of a sack of rattlesnakes.

"Good gosh!" cried Retch. "It's the Skragg boys! We're done for now!"

At the very least, I knew they would stop and grab our strings of fish, although my mind didn't dwell long on the very least. One of my worst fears had always been the possibility of being caught out on a lonely road by the Skraggs in a playful mood.

But the Skraggs roared right on by us, screaming a few vile remarks and laughing as they waved some rags out the window. It is perhaps human nature to regard persons such as the Skraggs as having displayed a deep sense of charity and decency, if they leave you alive and in not more than two pieces after an encounter with them. As soon as we stopped shaking, Retch and I felt those very sentiments.

"Gosh, maybe they're not such bad guys after all," I said.

"They didn't even take our fish," Retch added, his tone suggesting that the Skraggs had bestowed upon us a token of their deepest affection.

We plodded on up the road, discussing the recently discovered virtues of the Skraggs, until we arrived at Rancid's truck. The old mountain man was nowhere in sight. We sat down in the shade of a nearby tree to wait for him.

"Man, it's hot!" Retch said.

"Yeah," I said. "Except for missing Rancid, we could go for a dip in the creek and cool off."

"Psssst!"

"What?" I said.

"I didn't say anything," Retch said.

"Psssst! Boys! Over here, gol-dang it!"

We looked toward the sound of the voice. There was Rancid, crouched behind a bush.

"What are you doing there, Rance? You can't scare us."

"Ah ain't tryin' to scare yuhs, you idgit! Somebody stole all maw clothes! Ah got so dang hot Ah went crazy and took a swim in the crick. Felt so good, Ah couldn't believe it was water. While Ah was floatin' around down thar, some no-good yeller-bellied skonk stole maw clothes. Didn't mean nothin' to him, leavin' a feeble old man nekkid in the woods!"

Retch and I looked at each other. "It was the Skragg boys who done it, Rancid. The big ones. We saw Luke wave a pair of pants out the window when they drove by us on the road. They must have been in a good mood, because all they did was take your clothes. Didn't beat you up or anything."

"The Skragg boys?" Rancid said. "How many?"

"Five."

He shook his head sadly. I couldn't help but feel sorry for him, a pathetic old man who probably didn't even have another full set of clothes at home anyway.

"Retch and I'll just close our eyes and you get in the truck and drive home, I said. "We'll ride in the back."

"Cain't! The truck keys was in maw pants! Now here's what Ah wants you to do. You go off up thet little side road yonder and you'll come to Ike Munson's place. Ike died a couple y'ars back, and you ask thet pretty widder of his if Ah can borrow a set of Ike's clothes. Now git! The skeeters is taken after me somethin' fierce. Never should have washed off maw protective crust!"

Half a mile up the side of the mountain, Retch and I found the Munson place. The widow Munson was out stacking firewood on the porch. We explained Rancid's predicament to her. She straightened up and rubbed the small of her back. "Land sakes, if that Crabtree don't get himself in more trouble," she said. "I don't expect he'll ever tame down."

"It wasn't his fault," I said. "Can you imagine someone stealin' a feeble old man's clothes while he's in swimming?"

Mrs. Munson laughed a hard little laugh. "Rancid's turned feeble and old, has he?"

"Yes, ma'am. He admits it himself."

The widow Munson laughed her hard little laugh again and blew a wisp of yellow hair out of her eyes. "Well, I'm sorry, boys. I can't give Rancid any of Ike's clothes because what I couldn't sell I gave away. But I'll get something for him, even though he won't like it."

She went in the house and came out with a piece of clothing.

"I don't think he'll like it," I said.

"Beggars can't be choosers," she said. "This old blue dress is the only thing I can loan him. It'll at least preserve his modesty till he gets home."

We thanked her and rushed the dress back to Rancid.

"What in tarnation is thet!"

"It's a blue dress!"

"Gol-dang, Ah can see it's a blue dress! Ah ain't blind! Is thet all she had?"

"Yup. She said beggars can't be choosers."

"She did, did she? Wahl, gimme it."

Presently, Rancid emerged from behind the bushes wearing the blue dress. It was a little tight in the arms and hit him a good six inches above the knees. I felt an urge to laugh, but Rancid shot me a look that froze the urge right in my belly.

"This ain't the fust time Ah've worn a dress, ya know."

"It ain't?" Retch said, unable to conceal his amazement.

"Nope, it ain't. When Ah was a youngun goin' off to school one y'ar, the only decent outfit Ah had was a hand-me-down from the next oldest in the family, maw sister Clementine. A purty little dress it was, too, green with white poky dots."

"But didn't the other kids laugh at you?" I asked.

"Only once. Ah'm sorry to tell you this, Retch, but Ah got to borrow your vehicle." He then hopped on the bike and pedaled off, the blue dress billowing out behind him.

I grabbed my bike, Retch straddled the rear-fender carrier, and we took off after the old woodsman, who already was only a diminishing stream of dust in the distance. When we got to Fat Edna's Tavern a couple of miles down the road, there was Retch's bike parked outside. Fortunately, there was no sign of the Skraggs' big old sedan.

"I can't believe he'd walk into Fat Edna's wearing that blue dress," Retch said. "Why, the loggers will laugh him to death!"

"It's got to be humiliating for him, but maybe he was just so thirsty he couldn't pass up a cold beer no matter how much he got laughed at."

Big Ed Finch was just walking into the bar, and we followed along behind. Mr. Finch hesitated for just a second when he saw Rancid sitting at the bar sipping a glass of beer.

"Hello, Rance," he said.

"Howdy, Ed," Rancid replied, nodding.

Mr. Finch joined some men playing cards in the back of the room. They were all staring at their cards with great intensity. They must have been playing for awfully high stakes, because they didn't even seem to notice that Rancid was wearing a blue dress.

Fat Edna came down the bar and refilled Rancid's glass and set me and Retch up with a couple of orange pops. "I could loan you a raincoat, Rance honey," she said.

"Look like rain to you, Edna?"

"Nope."

"Than Ah guess Ah won't be needin' a raincoat. Thanks fer the beer. Ah got some bidness to attend to, so Ah better be off. By the way, anybody seen the Skragg boys around?"

"Yep," said Mr. Finch. "Saw that old sedan of theirs parked outside Bart's bar."

"Thank you kindly, Ed."

As Rancid walked out the door in his blue dress, I thought I detected a kind of *whoosh* in the room, as though everyone there hadn't breathed in a long time. It couldn't have been because of Rancid, though. He'd just had a bath in the creek.

Retch and I pedaled along with Rancid as he headed toward town.

"You better go on home, Rance," I told him. "I can rustle up some clothes for you. Besides, even if you find the Skragg boys and ask them to give back your clothes, they're not going to do it. Those Skraggs can be real mean."

"Thet's what Ah hear. But faint heart never won fair lady. And it don't hart none to ask, iffen you do it real polite."

When we reached Bart's Saloon at the edge of town, there was the big sedan, still parked out front. Rancid got off the bike, put down the kickstand, and shook the dust out of his blue dress.

"Now, you boys stay here," he said. "These folks might poke fun at me for wearing this here dress, and it would make me feel real bad for you to see such an awful thang. So you watch over the bikes. Ah won't be long." He walked into the bar, his long legs white and hairy beneath the blue dress.

"This is terrible," Retch said. "There's no telling what those Skraggs might do to a defenseless old man."

"I know," I said. "Maybe we should go get the police and—"

Just then a terrible crash came from inside the bar. A second later, two of the Skragg boys ran out the back door and around to the front. Then three other Skraggs scrambled out the front. They all piled into the car and revved up the engine.

"Good gosh!" I said. "That's all five of the Skragg boys!"

"No it ain't," Retch said. "That first guy out was Bart. There's still one Skragg left!"

At that moment we noticed someone trying to claw his way out through an open window, but he was dragged back in, squawling, "We didn't know they was your clothes, Crabtree! How was we to knooooooow?"

After that there was a long deadly silence. Retch and I waited, every so often remembering to breathe. Then the front door of the tavern swung open again, and Luke Skragg walked out. He was wearing the blue dress. Rancid came into view behind him, tucking the tail of a plaid shirt into a pair of black pants. On his feet were a shiny pair of boots.

Luke hopped barefoot over the hot gravel and squeezed into the car with his brothers and Bart. Rancid siddled up to the window, which Bart was frantically trying to roll up.

"Ah jist thought of somethin'," Rancid said, bending

over to look in the window. "Better give me back thet dress, Luke. It don't look thet good on you anyways. You jist don't have maw figure."

Luke wiggled out of the blue dress and handed it to Rancid.

"Thanks kindly, Luke."

The sedan roared off, spraying gravel against the wall of the bar.

Rancid watched the car until it was out of sight, his hands resting on the hips of his new pants.

"Be all right, Retch, if Ah borrows your bike a while longer?" he asked after a bit.

"You bet. Help yourself, Rance."

"You're probably all tuckered out," I said to the old woodsman. "You want us to follow you home?"

"What's thet?" he said, as though momentarily distracted from a pleasant thought. "Oh, Ah guess not. Thanks kindly, boys, but Ah ain't goin' home right now. Got to return a blue dress. Besides, goin' home would jist be a shameful waste of a new suit of clothes, not to mention a bath."

Many years later, after I had grown up, I realized that Rancid possessed a quality that I couldn't put a name to when I was a boy, a quality that explained the restrained and solemn attitude of the patrons of Fat Edna's bar to the spectacle of a lanky old woodsman wearing a blue dress. That quality consists of a certain kind of presence in social situations, possibly what the French refer to as *savoir faire*.

Warped Camshaft

I HAVE DECIDED it's time for me to come out of the garage and fess up: I don't understand motors.

"So what?" you say. Well, if you say "so what," that means you probably live in a large city and eat quiche with Italian soda at little fern cafes and have relationships and try to be a sensitive, attentive, and warm human being. Hey, that's fine with me. But I happen to live in a small logging community. Around here, any twelve-year-old kid can diagnose a malfunctioning engine during recess and do a major overhaul on it during lunch hour. A male person who doesn't know his motors is likely to be regarded with deep suspicion, or worse. So up to now I've faked my knowledge of motors, and with considerable success I might add.

As a youngster, I learned to get by with a few simple phrases I picked up around the playground. A kid would say,

"I got to get home right after school and help Pop work on the truck. Wouldn't start this morning."

"Better check the plugs," I'd say. I didn't know a plug from a porcupine, but this response was always in the ballpark of mechanical mystery, even though it might imply that both the kid and his father were idiots.

"We did check the plugs! What do you think we are, idiots?"

Once a kid mentioned that his father had a warped camshaft. I laughed. The kid frowned, shook his head, and pretty much avoided me after that.

I thought it might be a good idea to add "warped camshaft" to my phony diagnosis of car problems. If a car clattered past, I'd say, "Sounds like a warped camshaft to me."

"The tailpipe's dragging on the pavement!" one of the guys would point out, none too gently.

"That too."

Somewhere in most vehicles there is something called a universal joint. The first time I heard the term I thought it was some kind of crummy bar and grill found all over the world. But it's something on a car. Whatever it is, you can get a lot of mileage out of "universal joint." Let's say you're on a trip and pull into a greasy little roadside service station to get the oil changed. The owner instantly sizes you up as an easy mark for a rip-off on unneeded repairs. All you have to do is say, "Hey, bud, while you have the car up on the rack, check the universal joint for me." Right away the guy will think you know a lot about cars and will be less likely to sell you an unneeded radiator flush, transmission overhaul, and a new rear axle. Obviously, you should avoid being drawn into a long philosophical discussion about universal joints.

My honest diagnosis of car problems consists of the simple statement, "It won't go." I walk into the house and tell my wife, Bun, "Call a mechanic. The car won't go."

"What's wrong with it?"

"I just told you. It won't go."

"Oh."

Bun knows even less about cars than I do. One of the secrets of a long and successful marriage is shared ignorances.

To be fair to myself, I must report that when Bun and I were young and poor, with four small children, I actually tried my hand at doing mechanical repairs on our ancient sedan. The Car, as we called it, didn't seem to mind all that much and continued to go, despite my efforts. Starting and driving it, however, became increasingly complex. After one of my efforts at tinkering with its innards, The Car required two people to get it started, one in the driver's seat and the other holding down a doohickey under the hood. The Car would roar to life with a fiery explosion, sending a great cloud of smoke down the street and the neighbors into their yards to see what had happened. This was during the days when folks expected the United States and Russia might be exchanging nuclear missiles at any moment, and any loud noise came as a jolt to the nervous system. As a result, The Car was thought to be the cause of several emotional disorders in our neighborhood. It started receiving hate mail.

Eventually, The Car required not only two people to start it, but two people to drive it. Bun was assigned to hold down the doohickey under the hood, and as soon as the car exploded to life, she would slam the hood, leap in the passenger side, and regulate the thingamajig while I was engaged in dealing with the clutch, brake, and gas pedal, and simultaneously adjusting the whatchamacallit. (If you're unfamiliar with thingamajigs and whatchamacallits, that's because cars nowadays don't have them. I'm not sure about doohickeys.) Then we would roar off down the street, waving at the neighbors, who were either waving back or waving the smoke away from their faces. The ones with the emotional disorders were easy to spot, because they would be jumping up and down in the smoke and screaming weird threats at The Car.

Such is the confidence of youth that, despite the complexity and precariousness of driving The Car, Bun and I would load it up with all our camp gear and the four little kids, and head off for the mountains nearly every summer weekend. When we reached the narrow, steep, winding road that led to our favorite camping spot, the kids would be in the backseat singing "Go tell Aunt Rhodie the old gray goose is dead" for the thousandth time, and Bun would occasionally join in, when she wasn't needed to help with the controls. My total mental and physical capacity was maxed-out in making the car go and keeping it on the road.

Then we would meet a logging truck and have to back up a quarter of a mile to the last turnout. I will not describe this exercise in detail, because of the horrors it brings to mind, except to say that I twisted around and concentrated on steering backwards down the rough and winding road at ever increasing speed, while shouting out directions to Bun. She helped worked the controls, the hand brake being her specialty: "Brake, *brake!* BRAKE!" I'd yell. "Thingamajig out half inch. Jiggle whatchamacallit. BRAKE! BRAKE!" In the backseat, the kids would be singing another chorus about the death of the gray goose. (I think The Car is why they all grew up with a love of camping and nerves of steel.) It's a good bet that had any of our emotionally unbalanced neighbors been in the car with us, they would still be comatose. Which reminds me of the stranded motorist we picked up on our way out of the mountains one day.

Driving uphill one has the advantage that the grade itself serves as a brake. The opposite is true driving downhill, where the grade serves as an accelerator. As a safety precaution, we always went downhill in what was referred to as "low gear." This was exceedingly boring, and the kids were always whining, "Can't we go any faster?" The Car, apparently sympathetic to this complaint, would wait until the next steep grade and then jump out of low gear, much like a jack-in-the-box, and with a similar effect on me. The car would suddenly zoom down the hill with me standing on the brake pedal and the kids yelling, "Wheee! This is more like it!"

One evening we were chugging downhill in low gear when we came upon a vehicle parked in a turnout with a man and woman standing alongside of it. The man waved us down. I stopped, not wishing to pass up an opportunity to offer my services. There is something about stopping to help a stranded motorist that gives one a certain sense of superiority. The reasoning goes something like this: My car runs, his doesn't, so obviously I am more intelligent than he is.

"I wonder if you can give me a lift to town so I can get a tow truck for my car," the man said.

"Sure," I said. "What's wrong with your car?"

"It won't go."

"I've had some experience with that particular problem," I said. "Maybe I'd better have a look under the hood." I loved saying that: "Maybe I'd better have a look under the hood."

"Be my guest," the man said.

"Oh, please don't!" Bun said.

I shot her a stern glance. She was trying to ruin my first opportunity to look under somebody else's hood.

I looked under the hood. "Uh-oh," I said. "Just as I suspected."

"What is it?" the man said.

"Your doohickey."

"Oh no!"

"Yep," I said. "You're going to need that tow truck after all."

The man slid into the front seat alongside of Bun, and we started off down the road in low gear. He introduced himself as Harold something and explained that he and his wife had been out picking huckleberries, had got lost, and when they finally made it back to their car, it wouldn't go. "My nerves are shot," he said. "Would you mind if I smoked a cigar? It will calm me down." Neither Bun nor I minded, so he lit up and almost instantly seemed to relax as he puffed away.

After a bit, Harold said, "We're going a little slow, aren't we?"

"Yeah," I said. "But we have that one long winding steep grade just ahead. We usually speed up when we hit that."

"Okay," Harold said. He leaned back in the seat and shut his eyes.

Then we hit the steep grade. The Car, seeing yet another opportunity to kill us, instantly jumped out of gear. I can't recall exactly what happened after that, because the three occupants of the front seat fused into a single blur of activity. I shouted out orders to Bun: "Pull thingamajig! Hand brake! *Brake! BRAKE!* Now the whatchamacallit!" Bun lunged about doing the copilot stuff, all pretty standard, but

Harold was screaming and swearing and seemed on the verge of hysteria, possibly already over the brink. He didn't seem to realize that Bun and I were engaged in a merely routine activity, and there was no time to explain it to him. Then, at least as far as I could figure out, Bun somehow got her arm through one of Harold's suspenders, and she and Harold got all tangled up together, and the suspenders came loose and cinched up around Harold's throat. I can't say for sure exactly what happened, but that's my best guess. Anyway Harold stopped shouting and swearing and started squawking something about choking. So I yelled, "Forget the choke! *Brake!* BRAKE!" Then we hit a big bump, and Harold and Bun got wedged under the dash and appeared to be punching each other. By the time we got to the bottom of the hill, Harold was clawing the suspenders loose from around his throat, the kids were still singing "Aunt Rhodie," and Bun was smoking the cigar, which seemed to have a calming effect on her, too.

"Everybody get ready," I said. "We're coming to the bad part."

The Car performed one last service for us that year. It caught fire three weeks before Christmas, and we used the insurance money to buy presents for the kids. I haven't felt the urge to look under the hood of a car since. It's better not to know what goes on under there.

The 400-Pound Pumpkin

MY GRANDMOTHER, A stout little old pioneer woman, had come west by wagon and never tired of torturing me with tales of her labors when she was my age. During winter she had walked forty miles to school and home again through snow eight feet deep and wasn't absent or even tardy a single day. During summer she single-handedly cooked for logging crews of 800 men, and then, after washing and drying all the dishes, she split up a couple cords of firewood. Now, in old age, her sole responsibility was looking after me, while my mother was away at work.

"And land sakes, Pat," she confided in me one August afternoon, "looking after you is the hardest chore the Good Lord ever thrust upon me as retribution for my sins."

"What sins are those, Gram? Anything I'd be interested in?"

"I should say not! The whole passel of 'em wouldn't hold

a candle to the atrocities you come up with between breakfast and lunch on an average day. Now what instrument of
the devil are you foolin' with?"

"Oh, this is Whomper, Gram, the world's most powerful
slingshot. I made it myself." I held up Whomper in all its
mighty glory: a forked, two-foot-section of trunk chopped
from a thorn apple tree, woven bands of rubber as thick as a
logger's wrist, and a leather pouch fashioned from whole
tongue of boot, all the elements laced together with baling
wire.

Gram shook her head. "If that ain't about the most
useless thing I ever seen, not counting yourself, of course."

"It's not useless. I use Whomper for hunting elk."

"Pshaw! There you go with your tall tales."

"I didn't say I ever got an elk with it."

"I should think not. Why, there ain't a man in the world
strong enough to pull that slingshot."

"Oh yes there is. Last year at the Loggers' Picnic, Rancid Crabtree shot a stone as big as a peach clear out of sight
with it. He said the strain laid him up in bed for three days
afterwards, but he actually shot Whomper." I was a little
hesitant to mention the old woodsman, my friend and mentor, because Rancid and Gram were enemies of long standing.

"You stop with your fibs, young man! Still, it wouldn't
surprise me none if that lazy old fool Crabtree tried such a
stunt, just to show off. Speaking of lazy, I've got a job for you.
Go get a hatchet and help me cut my punkin loose from the
vine. I told Crabtree I'd pay him a dollar to haul it to the fair
for me. He didn't want to, because it too much resembled
work, but his greed got the better of him."

Ever since I could remember, one of Gram's pumpkins

had taken Grand Prize at the fair. That's because pumpkins were judged on size alone, with no points deducted for ugly. This year would be no different. Gram's secret pumpkin fertilizer, its ingredients too disgusting even to mention, and no doubt why I let them remain a secret, had this year produced a gigantic orange monstrosity that was almost frightening to behold. It was the sort of pumpkin that could give a person nightmares: *Townsfolk flee for their lives as the orange monster rumbles down Main Street, crushing bicycles and overturning cars, the police firing their guns into it*—Thunk! Thunk! Thunk!—*But the pumpkin, unfazed and indestructible, rumbles relentlessly on toward the grade school!* (Some nightmares are better than others.)

Gram's pumpkin, a great hideous blob of orange, must have weighed at least 400 pounds. The two of us couldn't budge it so much as an inch. With Gram shouting orders and threats, I chopped through the thick, sinuous vine, half-afraid that I was turning the pumpkin loose on an unsuspecting populace.

Gram smiled down at her pumpkin, then frowned at me. "If you wasn't such a slothful little critter, you could have grown something for the fair yourself, or even made something for the children's crafts."

"Like what, one of those milk stools, where they take two pieces of two-by-four and nail them into the shape of a *T*? Hey, maybe I'll enter Whomper. I bet he'd win something."

"Good grief!"

Just then we heard the sound of a truck driving up and stopping on the other side of the house.

"I'll bet that's Rancid now," I said.

Gram sniffed the air. "Yep, that's him all right. I reckon he forgot his bath again last year. That makes about five years runnin'."

Rancid came moseying out to the garden. He bit off a chaw of tobacco as he stared down at Gram's pumpkin. "Wahl, iffen thet ain't the gol-durn ugliest punkin you've come up with yet, old woman, Ah'll eat maw hat and throw in maw suspenders besides. You must be breakin' a law of some sort, growin' a thang like thet. Ought to be ashamed of yer-sef."

"Oh, what does an old reprobate like you know about punkins, or anything else for that matter?" Gram growled at him. "You want that dollar or not?"

"Spect Ah do. Ah'll winch the monster up onto maw truck, but iffen it tries to grab me, Ah'm cuttin' her loose, dollar or no dollar."

A couple of days later, Rancid and I went to the fair together and wandered around looking at the canning exhibits, the wildlife exhibits, and the various farm animals. "Ah likes the pigs best," Rancid said, reaching over a pen to scratch the back of a huge sow. "Pigs has got character. Ah kinda feels a kinship with them."

"That's what Gram said about you and pigs."

"She did, did she? Hmmm. Ah'm surprised she'd have a good word for me. You sure you're not makin' thet up?"

"Nope. It's what she said all right."

"Wahl, Ah'd say sumpin' good about her, too, iffen Ah could thank of sumpin'."

Just then a loudspeaker announced that the pumpkin judging was about to begin. Rancid blew thirty cents of his dollar to buy us each a hot dog, and then we walked over to the open-sided shed where a couple dozen pumpkins were lined up on a row of sturdy tables. We strolled along eating our hot dogs as we checked out the pumpkins, with Rancid still complaining about his purchase.

"Dang highway robbers," he muttered. "Thuty cents for two hot dogs. Git 'em fer ten cents apiece anyplace but the fair. They shouldn't even call it fair, if they's gonna cheat folks."

"Wow, look at the size of these pumpkins," I said. "There's some mighty big ones here, but Gram's still looks a little bigger than all the rest. You want to know her secret fertilizer formula, Rance?"

"Not whiles Ah'm eatin'. Hey, wait a minute. Thet biggest punkin ain't your granny's! Thet's old man Fleegle's. Chet Fleegle's. Ha! The old woman's got hersef beat this y'ar!"

"Oh no! You're right!" I gasped. "Mr. Fleegle's pumpkin does look bigger than Gram's. She's going to be so disappointed! You can't imagine how hard she worked growing that pumpkin."

We glanced at the crowd of spectators, always small for the pumpkin judging. Mr. Fleegle was standing back, arms folded, a confident grin on his face. Gram looked sad and disappointed. She didn't have to wait for the pumpkins to be weighed to know that the Grand Prize had at last eluded her. She now would be left with the embarrassment of a miserable and meaningless first.

"I can't stand to watch this," I said.

"Ah'm kinda enjoyin' it mawsef," Rancid said. "The excitement just keeps buildin' up, don't it? Hope maw heart can stand it."

"I'm leaving," I said. "I think I'll go enter Whomper in the children's crafts. Maybe I'll win Grand Prize and save the family honor."

"Ah wouldn't count on it."

We walked across a little open area to where the

children's-crafts judging was to be held. I looked at the competition. Nothing. I counted five two-by-four milk stools, along with a coffee table that could have been used as a small teeter-totter, a board that Richie McPherson claimed was a shelf, and several items I couldn't identify. Whomper was a cinch to win Grand Prize.

Barney "Fig" Neuton, the mayor, was in charge. A dozen spectators had already gathered for the judging.

"Is it too late to enter something in the children's crafts, Mr. Neuton?" I asked.

"No, you're just in time. Where's your entry?"

I pulled Whomper from the holster on the back of my belt. "Right here."

"Hey! That is some slingshot, Pat! Don't think I've ever seen a slingshot that . . . uh . . . that husky before. I'm sorry to tell you this, son, but you can't enter your slingshot in children's crafts. The rules say that any entry has to be useful. And anybody can see that slingshot is impossible to pull."

"Oh, come on, Fig," Rancid said. "Let him enter his Whomper."

"Can't do it, Rancid. Rules are rules. There isn't a man in the world could pull that slingshot, and you know it."

I pointed at Rancid. "Oh, but—!"

The old woodsman bent over and hissed in my ear. "Hush! I ain't a gonna do it fer you ag'in. One pull on thet durn slingshot lasts a man a lifetime and then some."

"But, Rance," I whined. "Our family honor is at stake! You can't let me down now!"

We both stared across at the pumpkin-judging contest. Four helpers were heaving one of the smaller pumpkins up on the scale. Mr. Fleegle's would be next. And then Gram's.

Mr. Fleegle was beaming brighter than ever. Gram was scuffing the grass with her shoe.

Rancid shook his head. "Wahl, since yer granny's punkin ain't going to win this y'ar, Ah guess I got to help save yer family honor." He reached down on the ground and picked up a stone the size of an apricot. "Hand me thet Whomper, Fig. Ah'll show you how a feeble old man shoots a slangshot."

Mr. Neuton shrugged his shoulders. "Oh, give it a try if you want, Rancid, but there's no way. . . ."

Rancid hauled back on Whomper, grunting mightily. Beads of sweat flew off his forehead. The spectators gasped, but some of them cried out, "Come on, Crabtree, you can do it!" And slowly, ever so slowly, the bands began to stretch and stretch, humming with tension, and finally, with one last mighty effort, Rancid pulled the slingshot to full stretch. A cheer went up. But then he staggered about in a circle, the slingshot at full pull, its bands singing, and spectators were ducking and dodging and falling over one another to get out of the line of fire. And then, suddenly, Rancid pivoted, aimed, and sent that stone sizzling across the little open area and straight into a 400-pound pumpkin! That pumpkin exploded like an orange bomb.

When I opened my eyes, all I could see was orange—an orange judge, an orange crew, orange spectators, an orange Mr. Fleegle, an orange Gram, and even a little orange dog who just happened to be passing by. Our own group of spectators stood in stunned silence. Then somebody began to applaud, and one by one the others joined in. Several men came over and slapped Rancid on the back and said it was the best darn show they had ever seen at the county fair.

Rancid handed Whomper back to the judge. "The boy's enterin' Whomper, Fig."

"Right you are, Rancid, right you are."

I tugged on Rancid's sleeve. "That was great, Rance, great . . . but . . . but . . ."

"But what?"

"You shot the wrong pumpkin!"

"No, Ah didn't."

"Yes, you did! You shot Gram's!"

"Of course! It wouldn't hev been right to shoot poor old Fleegle's and cheat him out of a prize he rightly desarved. Don't you see? If yer granny don't have a punkin, they ain't no way Fleegle's punkin can beat hers!"

"Oh. I suppose that's true. So what do you want to do now?"

"Wahl, fust of all, Ah'll spend the next three days in bed. After thet, Ah don't know. And Ah thank Ah'll git goin' right now, 'cause here comes thet orange old woman, hoppin mad. Probably'll want what's left of her dollar back."

I never knew for certain exactly why Rancid shot Gram's 400-pound pumpkin. Maybe it was just to be mean, as Gram claimed, or maybe it was an act of gratitude, for the nice thing she had said about him and the pigs. Whomper did win third place in the children's crafts, which was less than great, I suppose. But then again, our family didn't have all that much honor to save in the first place.

Tenner-Shoe Blight

I'M BECOMING INCREASINGLY concerned about my wife, Bun. She seems healthy enough, but I've begun to notice a pattern of mental lapses. For example, I was walking by the paper-recycling bin in the garage the other day and happened to notice the most recent copy of *The Old Outfitter's Catalogue*. I snatched the catalogue from the bin and went back in the house.

"Do you realize what weird thing you've done?" I asked Bun.

"Give me a clue," she said.

"Why, you tossed my new *Old Outfitter's Catalogue* in the recycling bin before I'd even had a chance to see it, that's what!"

"Good grief," she said, blowing on her freshly polished nails. "I don't know what could have come over me."

"No harm done," I said. "I managed to rescue it."

"I'm so glad. It's entirely possible the new catalogue contains some incredible outdoorsy thing you haven't yet purchased."

"You bet," I said. "In fact, there's lots of stuff in here I haven't yet purchased. Every issue comes out with a whole bunch of neat new stuff."

"Very thoughtful of the *Old Outfitter*."

"Yeah. But what I need right now is something basic—a new pair of boots."

"Ah, I see. New boots. I was under the impression you already had a warehouse full of boots and shoes."

"Not at all. You must be thinking of my bass-fishing warehouse. Either that or my fly-fishing warehouse. Nope, my meager supply of sporting footwear is stashed on a shelf in the shop. Come on, I'll show you."

We went out to the shop and I pointed to the shelf. "There, see for yourself, I can barely keep myself properly shod. Any other modern-day sporting person would laugh himself sick at my meager collection."

"You're right, I suppose," Bun agreed. "But only if the modern-day sporting person were Imelda Marcos!"

"What are you saying! All the footwear I have consists of my cowboy boots, rock-climbing boots, insulated hunting boots, uninsulated hunting boots, hip waders, chest waders, wading shoes, gum boots, leather-topped rubber boots, leather-topped rubber shoes, rafting shoes, boating shoes, jogging shoes, walking shoes, golf shoes, bowling shoes, moccasins, downhill ski boots, cross-country ski boots, snowmobiling boots, snowshoe pacs. And that's about it!"

"Why, you're practically on the verge of going barefoot.

By all means, get another pair of boots. But first of all, throw away that ratty old pair of shoes over there. They're absolutely disgraceful."

"What! My Tenners? Are you kidding me? I'm going to have those bronzed."

The shoes Bun had indicated with such a tone of disgust, if the nasal quality produced by holding one's nose can be considered a tone of disgust, why, those shoes were the ultimate in footwear when I was growing up. In those days, all the sporting activities engaged in by my associates and me were accomplished in Tenners. We called them Tenners after the man who had invented them, a genius by the name of Mr. Tenner. Once a rich kid from town tried to tell us that they were actually Tennis shoes, but no one had even heard of a Mr. Tennis. We laughed ourselves sick over the sheer ignorance of that kid.

The wonderful thing about Tenners was that you could use them for camping, mountain climbing, fishing, just about anything you had a mind to do. The Tenners were particularly good for fishing in icy water in the early spring. They were a little cool at first, it's true, but after ten minutes or so, all feeling left your feet and much of your legs, and you could wade a rocky stream on the sides of two broken ankles if you had to, and not feel the slightest discomfort. Mr. Tenner knew what he was doing.

We never threw our Tenners away either, usually because over the months of spring, summer, and early autumn they would gradually biodegrade, until at some point there would be nothing left of them. There was an almost imperceptible point of final disintegration. At one moment you would be wearing your beloved Tenners and the next you would be barefoot. Some guys went barefoot for hours without realizing their Tenners had disappeared.

In those wild and carefree days of constant hiking and camping and fishing, we would sometimes wear our Tenners for days without once taking them off. Some of the guys even prided themselves on how long they could go without removing their Tenners. One time my cousin Buck, who was about five years older than I, got into a contest with Ben Clevis to see who could wear his Tenners the longest. Buck won.

That was when we discovered the shoe's single flaw. Buck's toes had grown together, or so it seemed from the looks of them, which I won't describe, except to say they were pretty interesting as far as toes go. My aunt Sophie, Buck's mother, was horrified by the sight of those toes, and Buck wasn't too thrilled either.

"You get yourself over to old Doc Mange and have him do something about those toes," Aunt Sophie told Buck. Old Doc Mange had never been known actually to cure anybody of anything, but he worked cheap, and therefore was highly thought of as a physician in that particular time and place. I went along with Buck to give him moral support and comfort.

"What do you suppose Doc Mange is going to do about your toes, Buck? Maybe he will cut them off. If he does cut them off, maybe he'll let us keep them and we can put them in an empty coffee can and charge kids a quarter to look at them."

"Shut up! He ain't going to cut off my toes."

"Whatever he does, it's probably going to hurt a lot, Buck, to get those toes separated. Doc Mange took a big sliver out of my foot, and that hurt like the dickens. He didn't give me any ether or anything. We were at the Loggers' Picnic, and Doc had two loggers hold me down, while he cut that sliver out with a pocketknife he heated up to red-hot with a match. I almost yelled."

"*Almost* yelled, you little sissy! If I know you, and I do, you woke every dog in town and set them to howling their heads off. Now me, even if it does hurt, which it probably won't, I'll just laugh and joke with Doc all the time he's fixin' up my toes."

"I bet not, Buck."

"Ha!"

I finally decided there was no use in me trying to comfort Buck, because he was just too thickheaded to recognize when someone was trying to do him a kindness.

Doc Mange's office was in the back of his house. We arrived just as he was finishing his lunch. Doc wiped his mouth on his sleeve, plucked a cigar stub out of an overflowing ashtray, lit it, and then peered at us over his little wire-frame glasses.

"So, boys, what can I do for you? Another sliver, Pat?"

"Nope, Doc, it's Buck this time. His toes have grown together from wearing his Tenners too long."

"Will you shut up!" Buck snapped at me. "It really ain't much, Doc. Maybe you can give me a little ointment for my toes, something to free 'em up a bit."

"Take off your slippers, son, hop up on my table, and let me have a look at them toes."

Buck did as he was told. I could see he was none too happy to be sitting on what both he and I assumed was the operating table. Doc bent over and looked at the offending toes.

"Whewee!" he said. "Good thing I finished my lunch

before these toes showed up. Could ruin a man's appetite, that's for sure."

"You think you might have to cut them off, Doc?" I asked.

Doc studied the toes, a serious expression on his face, although not as serious as the one on Buck's.

"Nope, I don't reckon I'll have to do anything that extreme," he said, straightening up and taking a puff on his cigar.

"There, ain't that exactly what I told you?" Buck said, shooting me a smug look.

"Lay back down on the table and relax, Buck," Doc told him. "I'll get you fixed up in a jiffy." He pulled a big leather strap out from under the table and fastened it snugly across Buck's legs just above the ankles. He then fastened another strap across Buck's chest.

"Afraid I might fall off the table, Doc?" Buck joked.

"Hmmm?" Doc said. "Fall off the table? Oh, right, ha ha!"

Buck winked at me. I winked back. This could be good.

"I suppose you use those straps when you don't have a couple of loggers handy, huh, Doc?" I said.

"What's that, Pat? Loggers? Oh yes, I remember now, loggers. That's a good one, son. Nope, can't have loggers hangin' around to assist me every time I have to operate. Heh heh."

I winked at Buck. He didn't wink back. "Wait!" he yelped. "Hold up a second there, Doc. I think maybe if I give my toes a lot of fresh air, they'll probably heal right up on their own. They're startin' to feel a lot better already, as a matter of fact."

"Not good enough, Buck. Now, stop your frettin'. This won't take but a few minutes."

Before the operation got started, Buck and I watched Doc take some little cotton balls out of a box. "I hope you ain't thinkin' of stuffing that cotton between my toes, Doc," Buck said nervously, "because my toes are mighty tender."

Doc knocked the ash off his cigar. "Don't worry, Buck, these ain't fer you." He then stuffed a ball of cotton in each of his ears. Buck said later that's when he got concerned.

I thought it a rather bad sign myself, and ever since have wished I had asked Doc for some cotton to stuff in my own ears. Otherwise, I might not have suffered the hearing impairment that later kept me out of the Air Force. It's the sort of safety precaution you would expect a doctor to provide a young and interested observer of a medical procedure, but I suppose Doc's attention was focused mostly on his patient.

After these preparations were completed, Doc took a short length of hemp rope and calmly sawed it up and down between Buck's toes, until they were once again detached from their neighbors and cleaned up nice and raw. My hearing probably wouldn't have been irreversibly damaged from this phase of the treatment, but then, after all the toes were on their own again, Doc got a bottle of clear liquid off a shelf, and said to Buck, "Just about got you fixed up, young fella. My magic formula here will heal them toes of yours right up." He gave the freshly sawed space between each of Buck's toes a good dose of the magic formula, and I think that's when my hearing was permanently impaired. When we left Doc's house and headed home, all the dogs in town were still howling, but I was so deaf by then I could hardly hear them.

As we walked along, I told Buck that I had been enormously impressed with his performance.

"Shut up," Buck replied.

"Eh?" I said, cupping a hand behind my ear. "Anyway, I knew you were strong, Buck, but I didn't know you were that strong. You must have stretched that big old leather chest strap a good six inches, while you were trying to reach up and grab Doc by the throat."

"A couple inches more and I would have had him, too," Buck said. "Speaking of grabbing throats, you better never mention my visit to Doc Mange to anybody. You get me?"

"Eh?"

By noon the next day, details of Buck's toe operation, with emphasis on its operatic qualities, had spread to every corner of town. The chief suspect in the spreading of this vile slander was never apprehended, although Buck did chase him over two backyard fences, down an alley, and through a wrecking yard on the outskirts of town.

Doc charged Buck three dollars for the operation, which was a bargain, because after the rest of the guys in town heard about the cure for Tenner-shoe blight, they became foot-care fanatics and never again held a contest to see who could wear Tenners the longest without taking them off. Doc Mange obviously was a forerunner in the field of preventive medicine, but, like so many medical pioneers, he never got the recognition he deserved.

Letter from a Kingfisher

Much of the year I live on an island in a river, a few hundred yards upstream from a large lake. The island is connected to the mainland by a log bridge. The bridge gives the impression it's about to collapse at any moment, which is no reason to suspect that I built it. Age, as with me, is the villain of its deterioration.

A few years ago, a kingfisher took up residence on the bridge, or whatever it is that kingfishers take up. His primary interest in the bridge, I believe, lay in the fact that it provided the perfect perch for sighting in on the trout lurking in the deep and languid pool directly below. Every time I approached the bridge, the kingfisher would fly off, his manner of flight somehow conveying to me his annoyance at being disturbed. There was no reason for rudeness on his part, because he could have remained on his perch, and I would have driven past him without so much as a greeting. I had no intention of entering into a relationship with him. I merely wanted to get to town, buy my morning paper, and return. Passing the time of day with a bird was the furthest thing from my mind.

This is not to say that I dislike birds in general. For the most part, I find them to be interesting and even entertaining. From time to time, my wife, Bun, and I have gone to great trouble and risk in order to see and record the sighting of what to us at least was a rare and unusual specimen. Once, in Australia, we drove nearly a thousand miles to a lake for the purpose of observing the avian life that abounded there, at least according to our guidebook. When we arrived at what we thought was the place, only a sandy basin confronted us. We stopped at a nearby country store to ask proper directions to the lake. The lady at the store explained that we had indeed found the right place but the lake was dry.

"You should have come after a wet," she said. "All kinds of birds here then."

"When was the last wet?" Bun asked.

"Seven years ago."

So my bird-watching was just like my fishing. I should have been there seven years ago. The birding was fantastic then.

I offer that anecdote as evidence that I am in fact fond of birds, and will go to great trouble to seek them out. They, for their part, seldom cooperate. That is all right with me. I don't hold that against them. I have no wish to interfere with their lives, nor do I wish them to interfere with mine. The problem is that birds simply will not leave me alone.

Opening my cabin one spring, I found a dead duck in my fireplace. The following spring, I found a *live* duck in my fireplace. It remains a mystery how the ducks got into my fireplace, or why they would want to. Personally, I suspect space aliens put them there, but I don't know for sure. Removing a long-dead duck from a fireplace is a disgusting task; removing a live one is an adventure.

This summer a sapsucker took it upon himself to destroy Bun's fledgling fruit trees, the ones overlooked by the deer. Bun has a firm policy against my shooting anything on the island, but one morning at breakfast she looked out the window and saw the sapsucker at work on one of her trees.

"There he is again!" she cried. "Get your gun and blast that sucker!"

I explained that, provided my aim was better than usual, my twelve-gauge shotgun would remove not only the sapsucker but also the tree. Furthermore, because I have a policy of not shooting anything I won't eat, I did not relish dining on a bird whose main diet is tree sap.

I also put up with a couple of yellow-shafted flickers whose sole ambition in life seemed to be pecking my cabin out of existence. Then there was the deranged flicker who attempted to attract the attention of available females by drumming on my tin roof at five in the morning. I'd step out on the porch, hoping to frighten him to death, but he would only look down irritably at me from the roof and say, "What?" Because no reasonably bright female flicker would even consider this nut for a mate, he went on morning after morning rattling us awake at the crack of dawn.

"I'm going to shoot him," I muttered to Bun one morning as I clamped a pillow over my head.

"You better not. I think flickers are protected."

"Not him personally."

Apparently, the bird finally found someone dumb

enough to marry him, because he stopped drumming on the roof. If so, it does not bode well for the flicker gene pool.

Last summer I had an adolescent heron daily prowling the river's edge in front of my cabin, and when he tired of that, he would fly up and stand on the canvas top of my boat. (A heron is much worse than a gull in that regard, much much worse.) Most un-heronlike, he seemed not at all spooked by my presence. So one day I was staring out the window, preparing to eat a sardine-and-onion sandwich that I had just painstakingly constructed, when the heron stabbed down with his beak, speared some little furry creature, and devoured the poor struggling entity right there in front of me.

"Hey, Bun," I said. "How would you like a nice sardine-and-onion sandwich? No?"

But about the kingfisher. For some reason, I became attracted to him. There was something about that oversized head and ridiculous beak that I found appealing, possibly because he reminded me of a girl I dated in high school. He had such a serious demeanor, too, sitting there for hours on that bridge railing, frowning, intense, as though about to discover the secret of life. I wondered what it would be like to see the world through his eyes. Perhaps all would be brilliantly sharp colors and shapes, but meaningless, except for the flash and dart of fish down below. Fish would be his philosophy and science, his Aristotle, Kant, and Spinoza, his Einstein and Hawkin, all rolled into one.

I felt compelled to do something with the kingfisher. After all, he made his living off my bridge. I charged him no rent for office space. Surely he owed me something. I decided that the price for his using my bridge was an image of himself to hang on my wall, a photograph of him in all his solemn glory.

The bridge is a quarter of a mile from my cabin. Because he never ventured near my cabin, I knew I would have to snap him at his perch on the bridge railing, no major task. I clamped a camera with a telescopic lens onto the window of my car and drove down to the bridge. There he was, staring down into the water, the early-morning light illuminating him perfectly. Still well away from the bridge, I turned the car so that the camera would be facing him, and stopped. Seeing that I in no way posed a threat to him at that distance, the kingfisher instantly took off in annoyed and annoying flight.

The next morning I stopped the car twice the distance from the bridge as I had the previous day, with a telescopic lens the size of a whole salami clamped to the window. Before I could focus, the kingfisher flew off. Now I was getting mad.

The following morning, dressed in full camo, my face blackened with burnt cork, I snaked on my belly through the brush bordering the river, through a ditch only half full of slimy water, through a patch of thistles, and finally reached a tree from which I could snap a dozen photos without the kingfisher's having the slightest awareness of my presence. Ever so slowly, I peeked with one eye from behind the tree to locate the subject of this photo op. The kingfisher took off in annoying flight.

After a week or so of attempting to photograph this irritating bird, I gave up and resumed my daily pattern of driving over the bridge and watching him swoop off a moment before my tires hit the decking. Winter came, and I returned to my home in the city, without an image of the kingfisher to hang on my wall. When I returned in the spring, I noticed he wasn't on the bridge, but I really didn't care. Here I had tried to form a meaningful relationship with him, only to be rebuffed. So be it. I opened up the cabin and then went outside to see what if anything the deer and elk had left of the orchard—not much. As I tramped through the remnants of snow between the river and the cabin, I noticed something dark on the ground. I walked over and nudged the feathered shape with my foot, suddenly revealing the oversized head and the ridiculous beak. The kingfisher. I wondered what had finally brought him all the way down from the bridge. Never once over the years had I ever seen him anywhere near my cabin. And now, here he was, much the worse for wear. And then I realized he had used himself as a letter to me:

Dear Pat,

This is to let you know that I am dead. We had some good times at the bridge, didn't we, with you trying to sneak up on me with your camera and me always flying off at the last moment before you could click the shutter? It was fun. I knew when you noticed I wasn't at the bridge this spring you would wonder what had become of me. This is what did.

Sincerely yours,
George

George?

The Ultimate Bull

L ET ME BEGIN by saying that I don't hold with lying. It is a disgusting habit, with no other purpose than the deceit of one's fellow man and woman. After a lifetime spent in the company of elk hunters, I am pleased to report that they as a group abhor lying as much as I do. Oh sure, elk hunters are only human, and occasionally an innocent little fib will escape their lips while they're relaxing around the campfire of an evening.

A hunter might, for example, describe his packing of an elk quarter up a mildly steep hill in terms more appropriate to carrying a refrigerator up the north face of the Matterhorn. But that is an exaggeration to be forgiven. What cannot be forgiven is the outright lie, such as changing a five-point rack into an eight-point rack. That sort of unconscionable falsehood offends the honor of all elk hunters, who know that it is permissible to add only two points at most to a rack, and then only to a hunter's first elk. His future elk are not permitted to grow any points at all after they have been shot, unless, of course, the hunter has reached the age of sixty-five, and then anything goes.

I know an elk hunter who upon turning sixty-five gave up the sport. Scarcely a month later, he had bagged at least a dozen more elk than I had been aware of, which was three, and I was both pleased and astonished to hear of his recent good fortune.

"Ed," I said to him, "I never realized you were such a successful elk hunter."

"Yes, I am," he replied simply.

"Here all the years we've known each other, you have only mentioned three elk. Now, suddenly, there are eighteen."

"Twenty-three."

"Ah, twenty-three now. I would have thought an even two dozen perhaps."

"I prefer the odd number. Besides, I'm too old to hunt down another elk."

"Really?" I said. "Why, I would judge that the last twenty elk were about the easiest ever taken in the entire history of hunting."

"Well, they were a heck of a lot easier than the first three, I can tell you that."

By age seventy, Ed was kicking himself for not having at least ten of his elk officially scored, because they would easily have made Boone & Crockett, with several possible world records.

Ed was a man of restraint, however, and once his lifetime score reached twenty-three elk, he held pat on that number and refused to exceed it, even though that would have been easy enough for a hunter of all the skills he'd acquired since giving up the hunt. Ed did not believe in excess.

One day as he was approaching ninety years, I asked him if he had bagged any of those elk with a bow.

"Not at the present time," he said.

So right there you can see how modest he was. He could just as easily have shot half those elk with a bow, but he wouldn't do it.

As I say, all true and honorable elk hunters under age sixty-five, and a few over, abhor the lie and will never use it to deceive their fellow elk hunters. What means are left, then, with which to deceive fellow elk hunters? Disinformation. Yes, disinformation. This is a wonderful rhetorical device developed by the folks in Washington, D. C., to avoid telling either lies or the truth. Here's an example of how disinformation can be put to good use by elk hunters.

Let us say that you got your elk last year by grace of your cow permit. You are now playing cards with some other elk hunters, and one of the guys asks you if you got your elk last year. You feel no pressing need to mention that your elk was a cow.

"Yup," you say. "Whose deal is it?"

"Harry's. Good rack?"

"Nothing I'd hang on the wall. I thought Harry just dealt. It must be George's deal. No? Well, let's see, I dealt two hands ago and . . . whoops! Sorry! Didn't mean to spill my hot coffee in your lap, Charlie."

That is how disinformation allows one to keep from telling a lie without telling the truth, augmented by a bit of diversion.

Now let's say that I am seated at a table at a Rocky

Mountain Elk Foundation banquet, and I in all my years of dedicated elk hunting have never shot an elk. Naturally, I want to appear as adept at hunting elk as my banquet companions. Otherwise, what am I doing here at an elk-hunters' banquet? I certainly don't want to be found out as an imposter. So what can I do? When all of the successful elk hunters of the previous year are asked to stand, I alone at our table remain seated. But I do not merely sit there. I also smile bemusedly. You can get a lot of mileage out of a bemused smile.

"No luck last year, hunh?" one of the successful hunters asks me.

"Oh, I looked over some pretty good racks," I reply, "but nothing I wanted to pull the trigger on."

The reason I didn't want to pull the trigger on the racks is that they were hanging on a friend's wall, and he would have been mad as the dickens. Thus no lie is involved in this response, as you can see. My response is merely a bit of disinformation. Nevertheless, I have left the impression that I have reached the discriminating stage of elk hunting where only the ultimate bull will do. Impressed by this response, my dinner companions lean forward attentively, hoping to pick up a few tips from a master elk hunter. I must then launch into something like the following soliloquy in my best authoritative tones.

"The thing to remember about your really big bull is that he's almost never going to be where you want him to be. So you have to hunt him where you don't want him to be. And that's the steepest, nastiest hole in the mountains that you can find. You spend half a day climbing down into that hole, and there's your elk. Or maybe not. If he's not there—and you want to remember this—then he's someplace else.

Most of the time, in fact, he's someplace else. Or maybe he's where you wanted him to be in the first place, but you are someplace else, namely where you didn't want the elk to be, and he isn't. That's pretty much the essence of elk hunting as I see it."

"Gosh, sir, how many elk have you got in your lifetime?" a young fellow asks.

"Not really all that many, son. Fewer than a dozen. [Like a dozen fewer.] But keep in mind, that I'm not going to take just any old bull elk that comes my way." [Like if a bull elk ever comes my way on roller skates, I'm not going to shoot him. Unless, of course, I think he stole the skates, which he probably did, because how else would a bull elk get roller skates? So I'd have to shoot him anyway.]

"What's the longest shot you've ever made?"

"I'd guess about six hundred yards." [Missed, of course.]

"Wow! What's your best rack, sir?"

"My best rack? Hmmmm, let me think. Yes, my best rack. Whose deal is it, anyway?"

"Deal? We're not playing cards."

"Good heavens, so we're not. I thought it was a terribly slow game. I must be at the wrong table. If you gentlemen will excuse me. . . ."

Now, here's a tough one. Suppose a friend asks you the location of your secret elk-hunting place. Your initial impulse is to lie: "What secret elk-hunting place? I don't have a secret elk-hunting place." But that would violate the elk-hunter's code. On the other hand, you know if you tell him your friend will invite all his cronies along with him, and they will chase all your elk into the next state. You could tell him to just buzz off and find his own secret elk-hunting place, but that would break the bonds of friendship, which would be all right, too, if the guy didn't hold the mortgage on your house on which you're behind three payments. So you must tell him.

"My secret elk-hunting place?" you say. "Henry, you are the only person in the world I'd reveal this to, even if you didn't hold the mortgage on my house, and you must promise never to tell another soul. Here's how you can get there. You drive up to the end of Jefferson Creek Road, and then climb to the top of Jefferson Peak. There's no trail, but just keep going up until you reach the peak. You can't miss it. Now, pay attention to this, Henry. Take a long rope. You'll need the rope to get down the sheer cliff on the other side of the peak. The rope will also come in handy for hauling your elk back up the cliff. Once you're in the valley below, you'll see another mountain off to your right. Climb that one. Take a left at the top."

"Good gosh," Henry says, interrupting. "Isn't there a road anywhere near this secret elk-hunting place of yours?"

"Whose deal is it? I just dealt, didn't I? So it must be yours, Henry. Oops, sorry! Spilled my coffee right in your lap."

My Greatest Triumph

Among the very best ways I've found to depress myself is to add up and evaluate all my personal triumphs. They turn out to be few, small, and insignificant, and usually somewhat questionable. I'm left to wonder whether they were triumphs at all. Take my recent purchase of a new car.

I started with a salesman. My sharp bargaining reduced him to whimpers and what he claimed to be an offer on my part so outrageous as to border on sheer fantasy. He said he would have to go check the price with his supervisor, who soon emerged from a cubicle smiling confidently. I reduced him to tears. He went and got the sales manager. I reduced him to hysterics. The manager finally told me that even though the price I demanded scarcely paid for the cost of the raw steel in the car, he would give in, if I would agree to a slight compromise. I went along with the compromise, but only so that a pittance of a commission could be paid to the salesman, whose wife was in the hospital with an incurable disease and whose seven children were going to bed hungry every night of the week.

We shook hands on the deal. I climbed into my new car, savoring yet another personal triumph, and started to drive away. That was when I glanced through the showroom window and noticed that the entire sales staff had their arms around one another and were singing and dancing, and the sales manager was throwing handfuls of cash in the air. It makes you wonder.

I can perhaps be forgiven then, if I seem overly boastful in relating my most recent triumph, which was not only monumental, but absolute. Indeed, I would go so far as to say that all triumphs past and future might well be defined by this singular achievement. It happened thusly.

I had been paid a handsome fee to travel to a distant city and deliver a luncheon speech to a group of businessmen. Although I hadn't been informed of the real reason for my speech, it soon became apparent to me that the businessmen had to a man been suffering from insomnia, and I had been brought in to cure them of the malady. Halfway through my speech, I noticed that the desired effect had been achieved, for such had been the curative power of my words that all present were dozing deeply and peacefully—this observation confirmed by a chorus of snores.

My work obviously completed, I slipped quietly from the gathering, into my rental car, and headed for the airport. Checking the rearview mirror to make sure I wasn't pursued, as sometimes happens after one of my speeches—usually by the person who paid me the handsome fee—I determined that I was in the clear, and slowed to the speed limit. I relaxed and began checking out the scenery, which, unfortunately, turned out to be nothing more than a bunch of scenery.

Then, as I was passing a wooded area, I noticed a gathering of men and a few women strolling about dressed in skins and fur and ancient clothes. Assuming this was a camp of investment bankers caught unawares by the recession, I started to drive on, only suddenly to realize that the gathering was in fact a rendezvous of modern-day mountain men. I instantly whipped into a parking area and joined the throngs of sightseers roving from exhibit to exhibit. I myself have always wanted to be a mountain man and this undoubtedly would be as close to fulfillment of that dream as I would ever get.

I checked out the blacksmith shop, the muzzleloader range, the archery range, several shops selling moccasins, tomahawks, and handmade knives and the like, and soon had exhausted most of the exhibits as well as my curiosity. As I was about to leave, however, I came upon a demonstration of ax-throwing, a common defensive ploy resorted to by mountain men and a few of the current residents of New York City, one of whom may have been the irritable, buckskin-clad person demonstrating the proper technique for throwing an ax.

I immediately got into the line of touristy folk interested in trying their hand at throwing an ax and sticking it in the butt end of a log that had been set up as a target. Pinned to the center of the log was a playing card, the King of Hearts, which served as the bull's-eye. The King of Hearts was in no danger, to judge from the way the hurtling ax either failed to reach the target, overshot it, or bounced off the log handle first. The mountain man made no effort to conceal his contempt for the marksmanship of the participants. After each failed throw by one of us modern folk, he would demonstrate his prowess by sending the ax flying at the log. Although the King of Hearts appeared to be in no danger from this expert either, he did make the ax stick with a satisfying *thunk*.

At last it was my turn. The mountain man sneered at my suit and tie, obviously pleased that through craft and intelligence he had managed to escape such evils.

"Here's how you hold the ax," he growled at me. "Get a good grip right here and . . ."

My stepfather, Hank, and I are going out to the woodshed to split some wood. I'm about twelve. "Gol-durn!" Hank says, picking up the ax. "Another broken handle. You must have done it. That's the third one in a couple of months."

"I know, Hank. It's the kind of wood they're making ax handles out of nowadays. Hit a piece of wood a little wrong and they bust."

". . . then you bring the ax back like this," the mountain man said.

I'm fourteen. Hank and I are walking through our woodlot in search of a missing cow. "Look at that stump there," Hank says. "What do you suppose chewed it up like that? Couldn't be a buck scrape, not like that. If it was done by a bear, I sure wouldn't want to run into the critter that can claw wood like that."

"Probably a bear, Hank."

"Could be. I'd chop a section out of that stump to show to the folks at the game department, if the ax handle wasn't broke."

"Now watch how I make my throw," the mountain man instructed me. The ax made a single loop and caught the edge of the log. "That's how it's done." He grunted with satisfaction, walked up, and retrieved the ax.

"I think I've got the idea," I said.

"Yeah, right," said the mountain man.

I stepped up and threw the ax.

Vern Schulze, Kenny Thompson, Norm Nelson, and I are trapped by a snowstorm high up in the mountains. We've been holed up in an abandoned trapper's cabin for three days. We're all about sixteen years old. During breaks in the storm, we go outside and try to amuse ourselves with one of our favorite pastimes.

The ax, flying toward the log target, made a graceful loop. I couldn't see the expression on the mountain man's face, because he had bent over to cinch up a thong on one of his moccasins.

The storm has let up and may be over. Kenny is pinning a wooden kitchen match crosswise on the butt of a sawed log. "What's the score now?"

Norm checks a piece of paper in his hand. "I've got six, Pat seven, you've got eight, Kenny, and Vern's got nine. If Vern cuts the match in two with his next throw, he wins."

"This is getting too easy," Vern says. "Maybe we should see who can light the match with an ax."

The mountain man had just straightened up from tying his moccasin lace when the ax completed its loop and thunked into the butt end of the log. A cheer went up from the spectators. Applause broke out.

The King of Hearts had been neatly cloven in half!

The mountain man scowled at me. I smoothed my tie and buttoned my suit jacket. "Beginner's luck," I said.

Then I couldn't help but smile—triumphantly.

Another Boring Day

IT WAS ONE of those hot, dreary days of summer that filled our neighbors on surrounding farms with dread. Almost anything could happen on such days. Sudden storms could pulverize crops with hailstones the size of golf balls, lightning could strike homes and barns and livestock, wildfire could sweep across the countryside, wells could dry up from the drought, Crazy Eddie Muldoon could become bored.

"I'm bored," Crazy Eddie sighed.

"Me too," I said. "Can't you think of anything to do?"

"We could build another deep-sea diving helmet and you could test it again in the crick," he said.

"Naw," I said. "I nearly drowned last time."

"We could build another airplane and you could test-pilot it off the barn roof."

"The last plane crash nearly killed both of us, remember?"

"Yeah. Maybe we could dig another big hole in the ground and use it for a wild animal trap," Eddie said.

"The only wild animals we caught in the last one was a skunk and your father."

"Too bad we had to catch them both at the same time," Eddie said, sighing. "Otherwise, I don't think Pa would have been so peeved."

"He wasn't just peeved, Eddie. He chased us for about three miles."

"Parents are so boring," Eddie said. "I suppose we could go catch a snake. That might be fun."

"We each already have a pet snake. What do we need another snake for?"

"This would be a utility snake. We'd use it just once and then discard it."

"We could take it over to Olga's house and show it to her," I suggested. Olga Bonemarrow was one of our classmates in third grade.

"That's what I was thinking," Eddie said. "Olga might like her own snake. Hee hee."

After a brief hunt, we caught a fairly decent snake and took it over to Olga's house. We thought surely she would find it of interest. She did.

"We got a little present for you, Bonemarrow," Eddie said.

"Oh yeah?" Olga said. She made a fist and stuck it under Eddie's nose. "You better not try any funny stuff or you know what will happen."

"We wouldn't think of it," Eddie said, smiling. He pulled the utility snake out of his pocket and thrust it at Olga. "Snake! Snake!"

"Oh, what a pretty little snake!" Olga said. "Can I really have it?"

"Sure," Eddie said. "We thought you might like it."

"Oh, I do," she said, taking the snake in hand and stroking it with a finger. "I guess this is a peace offering. Well all right, if you guys promise not to play mean tricks on me, I won't throw you down on the ground and twist your arms up behind your backs until you scream. Deal?"

"Deal," Eddie and I said in unison.

We walked back down the road toward Eddie's place.

"Rats!" Eddie said.

"Double rats!" I said. "We wasted a perfectly good snake."

"Yeah. I figured it for at least a couple laps around Bonemarrow's house. So, what do you want to do now?"

"Beats me," I said. "I think this is just going to be one of those boring days when nothing goes right."

We took the usual shortcut across the Millstead bull pasture. The bull pretended to be looking the other way until we were in the middle of the pasture and then charged. He had us in his sights but forgot to lead us enough, and we beat him to the fence by a good ten yards. No contest. The thing always to remember about bull running is that a tie at the fence is as good as a loss. We stood on the other side of the fence and watched the bull bellow and slobber and paw the ground, the usual bull stuff, which was mildly amusing, but we had seen the bull's whole repertoire before.

It was nearly noon. We went over to Eddie's house and had a boring lunch.

"What are you boys up to today?" Mrs. Muldoon asked.

"Nothing," Eddie said. "We're bored stiff."

"Good grief!" his mother said. Her hands shook as she poured us each a glass of milk. Mrs. Muldoon was a strange person, but not nearly so strange as Mr. Muldoon, whose face started to twitch every time he saw Eddie and me walk by with some of his tools.

After lunch we went out and sat on the Muldoon porch. "Maybe we could make a cigar by rolling up a piece of paper real tight, lighting one end, and smoking it," Eddie said.

"Naw," I said. "I already tried that. Hot smoke and flames shoot down your throat. I think it might be bad for your health, too."

We sat in morose silence for several minutes. Then Eddie said, "Well, we could always go paddle the canoe on the crick."

"Too dangerous," I said. "We could get hurt real bad."

"Maybe Buster isn't home," Eddie said. Buster was the big kid who owned the canoe. He claimed to have built it himself. The only hard part, he said, was painting the name on the side. Even I could have come up with a better name for a canoe, but he had done a nice job of lettering.

"Maybe Buster got sent back to reform school," Eddie said.

"No such luck," I said. "I saw him down on the crick a couple days ago, painting over the name on his canoe. I hope he comes up with something a little more catchy this time."

"Yeah, 'Property of Sunset Resort' was pretty dumb, even for Buster. Well, it won't hurt to go look at the canoe, anyway."

"I suppose not," I said.

We found the canoe hidden upside-down in some brush with dried-up cedar boughs piled on the top of it. Buster was nowhere to be seen. We lifted the boughs off and turned the canoe over very carefully, just to make sure Buster wasn't hiding under it. He had renamed the canoe "Busters," not a great improvement in my opinion, and the lettering was much worse. We found a note inside the canoe: "Deer pat an eddee keep yor grubee paws off dis canoo or i twist off yor heds an brake yor arms an legs sinseerly yor fiend Buster."

"Holy cow!" I said. "That's awful!"

"No kidding!" Eddie said, picking up a canoe paddle and checking it for balance. "Even I can spell better than that, and I'm only in third grade!"

"I meant the part about twisting off our heads."

"Don't worry," Eddie said. "It's not like we're actually going to use his canoe. We're just looking at it. Maybe we should slide it out into the crick a little ways, to see how it floats. A little water can't hurt a canoe."

My eyes scoured the surrounding landscape. Still no sign of Buster. "Okay. But just for a second."

We slid the canoe into the water. It floated beautifully.

"I guess maybe I'll sit on one of the seats," Eddie said.

"Okay," I said. "But just for a second."

Eddie sat on one of the seats. "Why don't you sit on the other seat?"

"Okay, but just for a second." I climbed into the canoe and sat down. The canoe began to drift downstream. "Uh-oh," Eddie said. "I'd better stick this paddle in the water."

Eddie and I never did understand how Buster got the impression we were stealing his canoe. We were merely sitting in it, drifting along, putting the paddles in water and pulling them gently back in long easy strokes, but certainly nothing anyone but Buster would consider paddling off in it. The long easy strokes were abandoned when we saw Buster running along the bank after us. Then we resorted to actual paddling, and did rather well at it, considering our lack of experience. In fact, I had the distinct sensation that the canoe itself floated several inches above the water, possibly the result of a powerful magnetic field created by our churning paddles.

We soon approached a shallow spot in the creek, where it was apparent Buster could wade out and grab us. By now we were wondering exactly what techniques were normally employed in twisting off heads. Did Buster stand on your body to keep it from turning while he twisted on your head, or what? Not wishing to participate in such a demonstration, no matter how interesting, Eddie and I decided to make our escape across land on the opposite side of the creek from Buster, who was now charging full speed toward the shallow crossing. Traversing the Millstead's potato patch, we decided the canoe had become more hindrance than help, so we abandoned it and took off on foot.

For all Buster's rage about our touching his canoe, one would have thought he'd be happy to have it back. But no, his interest in the canoe had dissipated to the point that he leaped right over it without even breaking stride. Eddie and I were now the main attraction. By the time we reached the fence at the top of the hill, Buster was closing on us fast. We threw ourselves under the fence mere seconds ahead of Buster. Our lungs bursting, our legs turning to jelly, Eddie and I ran on in our hopeless quest for survival.

"I gotcha now, you canoe-stealers!" Buster shouted at us. "You guys are done for."

Reaching the fence on the far side of the pasture, Eddie and I sagged to the ground, turned, and watched the unrelenting Buster trot toward us. Even though he was still in the middle of the pasture, we could see sweat streaming off his face and his mouth gasping for air. But still he came.

To judge from the bull's expression, he could scarcely believe his good fortune. Here was a slow-moving, exhausted target right out in the middle of his own pasture. And the target hadn't even noticed him yet. The bull adjusted his crosshairs, pawed a cloud of dirt into the air with each front hoof, and pulled the trigger.

Buster, seeing that we had stopped, slowed to a walk as he came toward us, grinning, and making menacing twisting gestures with his hands. Not wishing to see even Buster transformed into Hamburger Surprise before our eyes—neither Eddie nor I had a particularly strong stomach—we pointed toward the bull, a four-legged Guernsey locomotive roaring down on the unsuspecting victim. Buster glanced casually in the direction of our pointing, as though expecting a trick. His eyeballs shot out a good six inches and snapped back, somewhat on the order of the paddleball an aunt had given me for Christmas.

The big slobbering beast circled the pasture twice, with the bull about three feet behind him, and then vaulted the fence at the far end of the pasture. The bull, in fact, had proved to be a marvelous stimulant to the exhausted Buster. It was the sort of thing you would like to turn into pills and sell as a cure for lethargy. You could make a fortune on it. "I got to take one of my Crazed Bull Pills now," an old person would say, and then he would leap out of his rocker and sprint ten times around the old folks home. I know that would be the case, because one glance at the bull erased every bit of Buster's weariness. Why, you would think he had just stepped out of a cold shower after a good night's sleep, he was suddenly so filled with vim and vigor. Even the bull seemed impressed.

Eddie and I wandered off in the general direction of my house. We came across a good snake, but it recognized us and slithered under a stump pile before we could grab it. I had a sister who wasn't of much use, but she could provide a bit of entertainment, mostly fancy dancing and loud noise, if you showed up with a snake. She was no Olga Bonemarrow. I used my pet snake, Herbie, on her from time to time, but I felt too much excitement wasn't good for a young snake and had to ration him and use him only on special occasions. Herbie always seemed limp and worn-out after a performance, but elated, too, over a job well done.

"I wish we had poisonous snakes around here," Eddie said.

"Yeah, me too," I said. "Rattlesnakes would be good. Or cobras."

"Pythons would be better."

"Yeah, I've always liked pythons. You could have a lot of fun with a python."

Mom was sitting on the back porch shelling peas when we arrived.

"What have you boys been up to?" she asked.

"Nothing," Eddie said.

"Just another boring day," I said.

"No kidding!" Eddie said. "I don't think I've ever been this bored in my whole life."

"Good grief!" my mother said, shelling some peas onto the ground. She was a little strange herself.

The Complete Curmudgeon

TRAMPING ABOUT MY woods the other day, I came upon a murder of crows *(Corvus brachyrhynchos),* an unkindness of ravens *(Corvus corax)* and even a convocation of bald eagles *(Haliaeetus leucocephalus),* if I may be forgiven for using the proper group and Latin names for these species, ahem. Now that I regard myself as a serious birder, I no longer use the more common term for such groups—"a bunch of birds"—as was my practice before becoming a serious birder. As it happened, all of the aforementioned groups caused me no little irritation, because I was engaged at the time in not mere avian observation but in a pursuit of a more practical nature, namely looking for a ruffed grouse *(Bonasa umbellus)* for my supper. And all I found were bunches of other birds, inedible at that, most of which seemed to take keen delight in my disappointment, or so I judged from their raucous screeching and squawking. When I at last tromped grouseless into my house,

I discovered a gossip of women *(Chatterus adinfinitus)* at my dining-room table, said gossip consisting of my daughters and their mother.

"It's only the curmudgeon," I heard one of them say. "No cause for alarm."

The curmudgeon! Why any of them would suppose that my neighbor Al Finley would come barging into the house without so much as knocking was beyond me, although I thought the possibility might bear some further reflection.

"It is only I," I snapped.

"Yes," my wife, Bun, replied, "the curmudgeon— *Grouchus crankeeyus.*"

This pitiful attempt at wit gave rise to such an outburst of mirth from the women that I could only surmise that their previous discussion, if such chatter can be dignified by the term, had consisted of comic accounts of my efforts to become a serious birder, no doubt zeroing in on my practice of casually dropping a scientific bird term into a conversation:

"I glance up at this flock of pigeons flying over," my friend Retch Sweeney tells me, "and, *smack,* right in the eye!"

"Columba fasciata," I say.

"No kidding, man! That pigeon must have weighed five pounds!"

The term I wish to consider here, however, has nothing to do with birding, except perhaps tangentially. It is *curmudgeon,* as applied to me by my spouse, Bun, albeit in a strained reach for humorous effect.

To escape the prattle of my spouse and offspring, I stomped mutteringly off to my study, formerly known as the "hole under the stairs," packed myself a pipe, ignited it, and, grinding the stem between my teeth, pulled a dictionary off the shelf and looked up *curmudgeon.* The dictionary defined the word as "an irascible, churlish person," which struck me as somewhat negative. Well sure, I may on occasion be a mite irascible and a tad churlish, but who isn't? I'll certainly admit to irritability from time to time, too. If the rough edges of life have honed my temper, they have also worn me down and exposed a few nerve ends.

I once overheard a woman simper to a professor friend of mine, "Why, Mary Ann, you used to be such a bubbly person and you aren't anymore." To which Mary Ann growled in reply, blowing a wisp of hair from her weary eyes, "I got too old to bubble." The same thing happened to me, I guess. I got too old to bubble. But I do enjoy a nice grumble.

One of the things I grumble a good deal about is the current practice of explaining to youngsters. "Oh dear, Ronnie, I see you have broken the tip off of my three-hundred-dollar Number Five Loomis fly rod that I have protected with my life on numerous occasions. Sit down alongside me, son, and as soon as I sop up my tears with my hanky, I will explain how you were using my fly rod in an unacceptable manner, namely as a whip with which to flail the neighbor's cat. Do you understand what I am explaining, Ronnie?"

Back when I was a kid, parents never cluttered up a youngster's mind with explanations. We nevertheless came to understand with crystal clarity the parent's disapproval of our actions. "All I was doing was trying to poke my kite out of a tree with the old man's split-bamboo fly rod. Whewee! I won't do that again!" Although the kid seldom went into detail about his motivation for never again using his old man's split bamboo fly rod in such a fashion, it was clear that his parent had made quite an impression on him, possibly several. After a while, a kid just understood how he was supposed to act, what the rules were, with no explanation at all.

An explanation from a parent would have terrified us. "Holy cow," we'd have thought. "The old man's explaining something to me! We're all doomed!"

Even as an adult I hate explainers.

Plumber: "The reason your faucet squirts water all over the ceiling is you put it in upside down." I'm paying this guy fifty bucks an hour to critique my do-it-myself plumbing? No, I am not. I am paying him to make the faucet squirt into the sink.

All people who actually know how to fix things are chronic explainers.

Doctor: "You're twenty pounds overweight. Your problem is eating too much and not getting enough exercise." And here I'd thought it was because the hole in the ozone layer was letting in too much gravity.

Sadly, explanations aren't limited only to people who actually know how to fix things.

Guy I've never seen before in my life but who sits beside me on a bus: "You know why the national debt keeps growing? I'll tell you why! The government spends more than it takes in, that's why!"

Me: "Let me off at the next corner, Driver."

Another thing that makes me irascible and churlish is positive thinking. It's so depressing.

Positive thinker: "The mechanic is smiling. That must mean there's nothing wrong with my car. I knew all along we'd be able to use our life savings to send Leonard to college."

Another positive thinker: "Just think, Martha, in three or four years we'll be harvesting apples off that little sapling we just planted." What this positive thinker refuses to accept is that his little tree will have to survive insects, disease, drought, heat, and cold before it produces a single apple, and besides that, the night after the planting a deer will show and eat his tree.

The problem with positive thinkers is . . . oh, sorry about that. I almost committed an explanation.

Something else that piques my irascibility is clothing manufacturers. I have stashed in the back of my closet what I refer to as Mafia shirts. By this I don't mean shirts that look as if they might be worn by the Mafia, black shirts to go with their white ties, but shirts made by companies owned by the Mafia. As you open the clear plastic package, you notice that exposure to air causes the collar to fray. According to the neck size imprinted on the inside of a collar that actually reaches around your neck, you should be playing offensive tackle in the NFL. But you still have the same ridiculously skinny neck you've always had. Shirttails have been bobbed so short they can scarcely be tucked beneath your belt, and men now have to wear suspenders to keep their pants hitched up to just beneath their armpits in order to keep their shirttails tucked in. It's true. Buttonholes are made one size smaller than the buttons, so that once you finally get the buttons fastened, you can't get them unfastened. You have to get the shirt dry cleaned while you're still wearing it. ("Easy with the steam press, Fu. *Yowwwwwww!* Thanks, buddy, what's the charge?") I don't want even to think about Mafia pants.

Boy, here's something that really burns me—those little clickers in cars that are supposed to remind you your turn signal is still on but the clicker is just loud enough that your wife, the passenger, can hear it but you can't, even though you're sitting closer to the clicker than she is. "Your turn signal is still on, dear," she says, her tone suggesting that this is because of a major congenital defect in you requiring either a frontal lobotomy or a hearing aid the size of a boom box. The turn-signal clickers in all the cars I've ever owned were obviously made by the Mafia in one of their shirt factories, where they were developing the seat-belt retractors that don't retract seat belts, so the belts get repeatedly stuck in the door and eventually start looking as if they had been chewed by a large dog whose intent is to kill you by remote head-on collision—the perfect murder. It is my opinion that the Mafia was also responsible for changing the headlight dimmer switch from a convenient button on the floor to a little shift stick on the steering column that has twenty-seven other functions, so that when you try to dim your lights you turn on the windshield washer, signal for a left turn into oncoming traffic, and set the cruise control for sixty-five miles an hour while closing on a tanker truck on a steep grade, and the approaching cars blind you by flashing their headlights because you still haven't dimmed yours, and then you almost collide with the tanker but manage to swerve out around it even as your frayed seat belt snaps in two, and then your passenger spouse says, "Your turn signal is still on, dear."

As I puffed my pipe reflectively in my den, it occurred to me that just about everything irritates me these days—the economy, politicians, positive thinkers, clothes, dams, clearcuts, spotted owls, young people, old people, fruit trees, deer, mechanics, plumbers, several major continents, and the expanding universe. I suddenly realized that, indeed, I had become a curmudgeon! The strange thing is, I rather enjoy it, I really do.

The Liars Club

Every morning before classes began, some friends and I would meet in the high school gym to exchange reports about our latest amorous adventures. Because neither I nor my friends ever had anything even remotely resembling an amorous adventure—we were mostly nerds—we started telling lies. This innocent pastime eventually developed into the Liars Club. Any member who lured the other members into believing a lie got to be president. The lie had to be told and believed while the club was in session, which was each weekday morning.

The presidency of the Liars Club remained vacant for months, because any comment whatsoever made by a member during the meeting was instantly met with rude expressions of disbelief. A member could show up in a full-body cast and claim he had been injured. The other members would laugh in derision. "Ha, you expect us to believe that? No way!" Becoming president of the Liars Club appeared all but impossible.

I should mention that my years in high school were served without distinction of any sort. Girls regarded me mostly as an obstacle to be darted around on their way to class. Coaches noticed me in the locker room only when they attempted to drape their sweat clothes over my head and shoulders to dry. The teachers were generally nice, jokingly referring to me as John or Richard or sometimes Melvin. As with so many students who pass through high school unnoticed and all but invisible, I craved recognition, or at least some small affirmation of my existence. For that purpose, I set out to craft and execute the perfect lie, the success of which would win me the presidency of the Liars Club and all the acclaim and glory that went with it:

"That's Pat McManus, president of the Liars Club," a beautiful girl would say. "Gee, I wish he wasn't dating all the cheerleaders simultaneously, because I'd love to go out with him."

"That's Pat McManus, president of the Liars Club," the coach would say. "I think I'll make him first-string quarterback."

"That's either John or Melvin, the president of the Liars Club," a teacher would say.

Okay, so nothing's perfect. Still, I had a lot riding on the lie.

I thought of various scenarios. I could pay Hulk Simmons a dollar to spread the rumor that I had challenged him to a fight. Once the rumor had spread, the guys in the club would be sure to ask me if I was fighting Hulk. "Yeah," I'd say. "He bumped me in the locker room the other day, and I called him out. Shook him up pretty bad, too."

"Wow, when's the fight?"

"Today after school, behind the Donut Dive."

"Ain't you scared?"

"Me? Naw. It's time somebody taught Hulk a good lesson."

I was about to set this plan in motion when I suddenly imagined Hulk walking up to me after school and handing me back my dollar. More likely, Hulk would walk up to me and not hand me back my dollar.

"Me and you is fightin' behind the Donut Dive in half an hour," he'd growl at me.

"You gotta be out of your mind, Hulk," I'd say. "You'd kill me in a fight!"

"I know. But it can't be helped. If I don't fight you, everybody will think I'm chicken."

"But if we actually fight, my lie won't be a lie, and I won't get to be president of the Liars Club."

"Tough. After we fight, you won't even get to be you."

It was a close call. I could see I had to come up with a plan that didn't involve Hulk Simmons and my getting killed behind a stupid donut shop. And I did.

One morning I arrived at the gym looking terribly sad. The club members were grouped together on the bleachers. "Watch it," somebody said. "McManus is up to something. Don't fall for that sad look. It's a trick." Everyone was on guard, the common expression of disbelief already forming on sneering lips.

"Anybody heard how Bob's mom is doing?" I asked, staring sadly down at my shoes. The members knew Bob was a good friend of mine and a rather studious fellow, whose hobby, incidentally, happened to be tinkering with explosives. He had even set up his own highly sophisticated chemistry lab. Nobody messed with Bob. Give him a playful punch and both you and he might go up. That at least was the myth Bob had carefully nurtured.

The members' faces began to harden with suspicion. Finally, someone asked, "What about Bob's mom?"

"Is she going to make it?" I responded, as though what I was talking about must be common knowledge. Beginning liars should take note that the opening I was using, now referred to among competition liars as the "McManus Opening," consisted entirely of questions, the implication being that my adversaries knew something I didn't. A question can't be a lie, but can serve much the same purpose. "Is she going to make it?" I asked again.

"Make what?"

"Live, of course."

Some of the faces looked puzzled. "Why shouldn't she live?"

"You mean you don't know about the explosion?" I said angrily. "You can't barely survive an explosion like that and be up baking cookies the next day, can you?"

Some of the faces turned solemn. A couple registered shock.

"He's setting us up," said one of the more accomplished liars, but there was a touch of doubt in his tone. He couldn't quite bring himself to believe somebody would lie about something this horrible and tragic. Ha!

I could feel the lie drawing them in. It was a big lie, a magnum lie, a powerful lie. I had known instinctively that a small lie wouldn't be up to the job.

"Didn't you notice Bob's house when your bus came by it this morning, Larry?" I asked. "Isn't it still smoldering?"

The membership turned as one to look at Larry, the bus rider, from whom I had requested confirmation. What I counted on here was the fact that Larry had absolutely no reason to notice Bob's house *any* morning, let alone this one.

"Gee, I dunno," Larry said, obviously embarrassed for not being more observant. "I never even looked at his house."

Voices in the background: "I know McManus is lying. . . . He asked Larry, though. . . . I don't believe . . . Why would he ask Larry if . . . ?"

"Do you mean to tell me, Larry, you didn't even notice that Bob's house is gone?" I demanded.

"I'm sorry! I'm sorry! I wasn't paying attention! Was Bob . . . ?"

Dramatic pause. "Yes."

I took out my handkerchief and wiped my eyes, the tears a product of my pent-up mirth, which also had strangled my voice into a pained croak. The effect on the Liars Club was marvelous.

"So far," I croaked, "I guess they've found only a few small pieces. A finger here, a toe there. . . . *Choke!* Apparently, he was holding the explosive when . . ." I was almost too overcome by emotion to continue. "His . . . mom . . . the . . . only . . . survivor," I croaked. "Even . . . his . . . dog . . . Spike."

"Oh no, not Spike, too!"

"Poor old Spike. Bob loved that dog."

"Spike" was a masterful touch, a stroke of pure genius. Bob didn't even have a dog, let alone one named Spike! And the membership *knew* Bob didn't have a dog! The lie had not only taken them in but reshaped their entire perception of reality.

"I still think he's lying," Harold said, but with no great conviction. "Look, there's Norm. We can ask him. Hey, Norm, come over here?" Norm was another good friend of Bob's.

Norm plodded across the gym floor.

"Is it true about Bob?" half a dozen voices asked.

"Geez," Norm said, his voice quivering. "It seems so unreal. I was just talking to Bob a few hours before the explosion."

Norm is one of the finest method actors I've ever known. That was why I used him for the clincher, the coup de grace. He had probably been up all night rehearsing his part and acquiring the dark puffy circles around his eyes.

The tragedy now confirmed, a tidal wave of grief swept over the Liars Club. Eyes welled with tears. Lips trembled.

"Gee, I thought it was just another lie," Harold said. "But it's true. Poor Bob."

"Just a few fingers and toes, hunh," Larry said. "Gosh, it was only yesterday I saw all of Bob walking through the gym on his way to—"

At that moment, the victim of the explosion sauntered through the gym on his way to class.

Bob seemed slightly puzzled and even somewhat concerned by the intensity of the stares directed at him, partly because I hadn't informed him he was to play the lead in the Big Lie. Then a great roar of outrage exploded from the Liars Club. Thinking he was about to be set upon by a mob of angry and maniacal liars, Bob fled the gym, leaving pages of homework fluttering in the air behind him.

I must say the other liars in the club did not respond graciously to my sudden ascent to the presidency. They were so enraged, in fact, that they disbanded the club on the spot. After all my effort, I got to be president of the Liars Club for only a couple of minutes. It was enough though.

A Couple Pickles Shy of a Full Barrel

I MADE TWO basic mistakes that day. The first was going fishing with Al Finley and Retch Sweeney at the same time. They can't stand each other, but I thought maybe a day of fishing together in a small boat would create one of those male-bonding things between them. My other mistake was renting a boat from Fizzy, owner, manager, maintenance man, and sole employee of Fizzy's Fishing Resort, which consists of a rotting dock and a half-dozen dilapidated shacks that Fizzy has the gall to rent as "cabins."

"You fellas renting a cabin for the night?" Fizzy asked as we unloaded our gear from the rear of Al's station wagon. "Only twenty-eight bucks. I throw in breakfast." He wiped a dribble of tobacco juice off his stubbly chin with a greasy sleeve.

"How much if you don't throw in breakfast?" Retch asked.

"Same rate either way."

"Well what kind of a deal is that?" Retch said. "I think we should get a substantial discount if we eat the breakfast."

"No cabin, Fizzy," I said. "We're just out for the day. All we need is a boat. You got one that's lakeworthy?"

"All my boats is lakeworthy," Fizzy snapped. "The only problem I ever have with these boats is from fellas who don't know nothin' about boats. Had two nincompoopers in here just last week, rented a boat and then abandoned it at the far end of the lake. Must have scaled that cliff, hiked all the way back through the woods and swamp, then sneaked their car out of the parking lot without me catchin' them. Durn fools!"

"Parking lot?" Retch said. "I didn't know you had a parking lot, Fizzy. How come we always have to leave our car on this pile of rocks?"

"This pile of rocks *is* the parking lot! Now you want a boat or you just gonna jaw at me all day? I got a bidness to run."

"Really?" Retch said. "What is it?"

I could see that Retch was feeling more ornery than usual, and that did not bode well for my being trapped all day in a leaky old boat with him and Finley. Al Finley, a banker, happens to be a fanatic about such things as proper etiquette, tidiness, order and reason, archaic concepts that, as Retch points out, don't even help you shoot a decent game of pool.

"Let's take a look at the boats," Al said, walking out on the dock. "I'm already putting my life at risk merely by going fishing with you two bozos. I would at least like to increase the minimal probability of my survival by finding a boat with only a modest similarity to a sieve."

We examined several of Fizzy's boats, rejecting one right off, for the reason that the only evidence of its existence was a bowline tautly disappearing into the water at the edge of the dock. We did, however, spend a few moments contemplating the straining bowline.

"Don't pay no attention to that boat," Fizzy said. "I'm just soaking it a bit to tighten up some seams. Now right here is a good sound boat."

"This boat?" Retch said. "You're callin' this boat sound, Fizzy? Why it's so old George Washington probably used it to cross the Delaware. But what the heck, if it was good enough for George Washington, it's good enough for us. We'll take it."

"You must be mad!" shouted Al. "Can't you see it's leaking? There's no way I'm going out in that monstrosity!"

Two hours later, Retch and I had each boated a couple of nice bass. "Can you believe that Finley?" Retch said. "Worried about a little water in the bottom of the boat."

"Yeah," I said. "I've been out here in worse boats. Hand me the bailing can. The trick is not to let the leakage get ahead of you. If Finley had known that, he wouldn't have been so nervous."

"Would you two bozos stop talking about me as if I weren't here?" Al said. "By the way, I think it's Retch's turn to row for a while."

The outboard motor had actually run for a good twenty minutes or so, just long enough to get us up to the far end of the lake. Then it had died, probably of a natural cause, old age being the best bet.

"Row us a little closer to shore, Finley," Retch said. "That looks like some good bass water over there."

"Oh, for Pete's sake, here we are adrift in a leaky boat and you can't think about anything other than catching fish."

"Got nothin' else to do," Retch said. "Boy, wait until I get ahold of that Fizzy!"

Without realizing it, I at that very moment started the horrible contest. "Oh, you won't do anything to Fizzy. You know he's not quite all there."

"Oh, I know that," Retch said. "He's been about half a bubble off plumb for years."

Then Al contributed: "It was quite obvious to me that his elevator doesn't go all the way to the top floor."

He rowed us along in silence, save for the splashing of the oars.

After a bit, Retch said, "Yeah, Fizzy's got only one oar in the water."

More thoughtful silence.

"Quite true," Al said. "You might even say that he's not playing with a full deck."

"Enough!" I shouted. "Let's all simply agree that Fizzy is a little bit off his rocker."

Retch and Al glared at each other in a manner reminiscent of old war movies about men adrift in a lifeboat, slowly but surely going mad. The sun beat down upon us, the oarlocks squeeked hideously, and our voices turned hoarse from thirst, there being nothing to drink but a lake full of water.

"Oh, all right, he's little bit off his rocker," Retch croaked. "But I'd have to say Fizzy's got at least one wheel in the sand."

Al: "He's one brick shy of a load!"

Retch: "He's got a bat in his belfry!"

Al laughed maniacally. "Fizzy isn't wrapped too tight either."

Retch sat for a long while, his brow furled in thought. "Okay, the problem with Fizzy is that his bulb isn't screwed all the way in."

"I've never heard that one before," Al said.

"That's because I just made it up."

"Foul! You can't just make up these insanity expressions!"

"Why not? Somebody makes 'em up."

"Oh, so you want to play hardball, huh, Sweeney? Okay then. Let me see. Hmmmm. I got one. His dipstick shows a quart low."

"His dipstick? You're the dipstick, Finley. That doesn't make any sense."

"What does sense have to do with this? Your turn."

"Stop!" I cried. "I can't take any more of this!"

"We're not stopping on my turn," Retch growled. "Let's see. Hmmmm."

I lay back with my head on the bowline and tried to block out the insane insanity contest. Then I must have dozed off, for how long I'm not sure. Suddenly, I once again became aware of the angry, rasping voices of Al and Retch.

Al: "His glue never quite set up."

Retch: "He's one bean short of a full can."

Al: "His anchor doesn't go all the way to the bottom."

Retch: "He needs an adjustment on his vertical hold."

Al: "His spin dry is one sock out of balance."

Retch: "The tail's too short for his kite."

Al: "His boat's leaking faster than we can bail."

Retch: "His fuse don't go all the way to the powder."

Al: "I said, *HIS BOAT'S LEAKING FASTER THAN WE CAN BAIL, YOU FOOL! WE'RE GOING TO SINK!*"

Nothing so stimulates alertness in a boater as the cry, "We're going to sink!" I responded in the traditional manner, which could easily be mistaken by an uninformed observer as a frenzy of bailing. It was several seconds before I realized I wasn't holding the bailing can, which had been snatched from me by Retch. Al was on his knees bailing with cupped hands, and I joined in with my own cupped hands. Pausing a moment to make a calm and logical assessment of our situation, including the standard comparison of one's endurance as a swimmer with the distance to the nearest shore, I noticed that the water in the boat showed distinct signs of current. I suspected that something basic had given way somewhere in the aft region of the rickety craft, a suspicion confirmed by the fact that but a few moments later the three of us were sitting in a boat submerged up to its gunnels. There was nothing to do but go over the side and, grasping the gunnels, kick-stroke our way to shore.

As we paused to take a breather, Finley propped both of his elbows up on the gunnels and gasped, "Well, this fishing trip with you two bozos is turning out better than I expected. At least I'm still alive."

"Don't blame us," Retch said. "It's Fizzy's fault. I always knew he was about half a twist off tight."

"That insight hardly qualifies you as perspicacious," Al responded. "Any fool could see he was one egg short of an omelet."

"Oh yeah? Well, I would have to say that Fizzy is—!"

I judged the swimming distance to the nearest shore

now to be about half a mile or twice my best swimming distance in recent years. Only a desperate person would even consider taking such a risk. I started off with a backstroke.

After I had scaled the cliff and was slogging my way through the swamp back to Fizzy's, it suddenly struck me: Al and Retch were both a couple pickles shy of a full barrel.

Excuse Me, While
I Get Out of the Way

MY COUSIN BUCK was a natural-born leader, and it was from him I first learned about the essential character of leaders, no matter how they are born. High-powered executives like to roar: "Either lead, follow, or get out of the way." I have Buck to thank for my becoming one of the people who get out of the way.

Buck early on displayed two of the most common qualifications for leadership, those being that he was tall and had nice hair. Furthermore, he was burdened with only minimal intelligence, which left him free to act without the usual restraints provoked by thought. And, finally, he possessed charisma, that peculiar trait of personality so magnetic it draws a leader's followers happily after him into the most desperate and stupid of predicaments, for which favor he earns their undying gratitude and devotion. Indeed, many a leader has won glory for heroic acts in situations that, except for his unrelenting arrogance and stupidity, would never have occurred in the first place. I will name no names, except that of Buck, who was just such a fine and heroic leader.

Although Buck's exploits as a leader still abound in my memory, I will select only one for the purpose of illustration, namely the expedition into Big Fish Lake, a tiny oval of blue we discovered on a map. We naturally supposed that the name meant there were big fish in the lake.

"No doubt about it, that lake has got some huge fish in it," Buck said as he and I perused a map. "Otherwise, the guys who made this map would never have named it Big Fish Lake."

"You must be right, Buck," I said. "By the way, did you notice that right over here on the other side of Lookout Peak is a smaller lake called Little Fish Lake?"

"Well, we sure as heck don't want to hike into that one!"

The expeditionary force consisted of five of us: Billy, Lester, Jake, and me, all in our early teens, and, of course, Buck, in his later teens. During our planning session, Buck explained that we needed to pack only modest provisions. "There'll be plenty of big fish for us to eat, men, plenty of big fish."

Because the lake was far back in mountains previously untrekked by us, I surreptitiously slipped the map and a compass into my pack, hoping not to be found out by Buck, who was of the opinion that such navigational aids were only for sissies. He liked to say the only map and compass he needed were in his head, and I supposed they were. They would not have been crowded in there, either, but could have stretched out and made themselves comfortable. Still, Buck's map may have been better than the one I packed, which was so deceptive in its untopographical simplicity it could show two points on a trail an inch apart and hide the Matterhorn in between them. As for providing useful information about terrain to be crossed, that map was about as closedmouthed as any I've ever seen. It slyly failed to mention swamps and mountains and cliffs and canyons and raging streams and numerous other unpleasant surprises. The map exhibited such homicidal tendencies that I was almost afraid to turn my back on it. But at least it was a map.

As was the common practice on our expeditions, Buck immediately assumed the position of leader, without the distraction of a vote by the membership. None of the rest of us qualified as a leader anyway, and for obvious reasons. Billy was too short, Lester didn't have good hair, Jake had excessive intelligence, and I wore glasses. The wearing of glasses in and of itself deprived a person of even the hope of becoming a leader.

The expedition set out early one morning along a well-maintained Forest Service trail that paralleled a sparkling stream flowing out of a narrow valley that extended back into the mountains. After an hour or so of easy hiking, Buck stopped and put his hands on his hips, always a bad sign, because it indicated he was attempting thought.

"This trail is getting us nowhere," he said, addressing us troops. "I don't know what the Forest Service could have been thinking when they built this trail. It obviously takes the long way around. We can save a half-day of hiking by cutting off through the woods here and climbing up that ridge to the mountaintop."

I stared into the thick tangle of brush and trees between

us and the ridge. "But, Buck, maybe there's a swamp or something out there. That could be why the Forest Service didn't build the trail off that way."

"If there's a swamp out there, I'll eat my hat," Buck said. "Swamps just don't happen at this elevation."

"I didn't know that," I said.

"Of course you didn't," Buck said. "Anybody who wears glasses wouldn't. Now shut up and follow me."

We followed Buck off the trail and into the woods. It was tough going, and we soon got separated. Clouds of deerflies swarmed about us, but were soon driven off by mosquitoes. My feet started getting wet. Then slimy mud began lapping my boot tops.

"We're in a swamp, Buck!" I yelled.

A dark, swirling column of mosquitoes just ahead of me yelled back, "This ain't no swamp!"

"I thought it was."

"No, it ain't."

Murky green water rose to my waist. Tattered curtains of moss billowed out from the limbs of silvery dead trees.

"It sure looks and feels and smells like a swamp, Buck."

"Well, it ain't. This ain't nothin' like a swamp. Now, everybody come over here. I just found an island."

Billy, Jake, and I struggled over to the island and climbed up beside Buck. While we ate sandwiches and sipped from our canteens, Buck took the opportunity to identify various birdcalls for us. The calls were from birds none of us had ever heard of before, so the lesson was very educational. One call sounded kind of a sad and eerie, a strange, haunting cry that seemed to hang in the air.

"That's your little Brown-headed Pine Bird," Buck said.

"You can tell by the way it sort of trills off at the end. You can't mistake it."

"I don't think so," I said.

"You don't? Well, just what kind of bird do you think it is then, smarty?"

"I think it's Lester," I said. "He always trills off at the end like that."

And sure enough it was Lester. He emerged from a cloud of mosquitoes long enough to see us and then came bounding through the water toward our little island.

"Oh, am I ever glad to find you guys!" he gasped, "I thought I would be lost in this swamp forever!"

"This ain't no swamp!" Buck snapped. "Boy, are you guys ever lucky to have me here to lead you. Otherwise, you'd have no idea where you are."

"So where are we, Buck?" Jake asked.

"Where are we? Ha! That's just the sort of dumb question I'd expect from you, Jake. I'll tell you where we are. We're here on this little island! Any fool could see that."

"But where is 'here'?" Billy said, looking around the watery area that appeared very much like a swamp but wasn't.

"I could show you where here is if we had a map, but we don't," Buck snapped. "The only map we have is the one in my head."

"I have a map," I said.

"You sissy!" Buck said. "Well, since you have a map, hand it over, and I'll show you all where we are."

I handed Buck the map, and he spread it out on the ground. He studied it a while, his brow puckered from concentration. "All right, Jake, here's a little test for you.

I bet you can't pick out the spot on this map where we are."

Jake looked over Buck's shoulder. "We have to be right here," Jake said, placing his finger on the map.

"I'll be danged!" Buck said. "You guessed the very spot. Yep, that's exactly where we are. As you can see, we are only about six inches east of Lookout Peak. We should be able to cover a measly six inches before nightfall."

"But we're west of Lookout Peak," Jake said.

"East, west, whatever," Buck said. "Don't try to confuse me with meaningless details. Follow me, men!"

"Yea, Buck!" we cheered.

We reached high ground an hour later and started the climb up the ridge. But the ridge didn't go up in a gradual incline toward the peak, as one would expect of any decent ridge. It moseyed upwards for a ways, raising false hopes in us, and then dropped off into a deep ravine, which we had to climb down into and then back out of—a half hour of treacherous climbing, and we hadn't gained a foot of altitude. The ridge found this little trick so amusing, it repeated it a dozen times before we reached the peak.

During one of our rest stops, Buck guzzled deeply from his canteen. "Might as well drink up, men. There's gotta be an icy spring up near the top of the mountain where the guy that mans the fire lookout tower gets his water. They always put lookout towers on the only peak around that's near water." So we all guzzled deeply from our canteens, and then, laughing heartily, we dumped the remainder of our water over our sweating heads.

"Yea, Buck!"

When we reached the peak, I couldn't see the lookout tower anywhere.

"Where's the lookout tower, Buck?"

"How should I know? It's got to be here someplace. Why would they hide a lookout tower?"

"I see a lookout on that peak way over there," Billy said. "Strange that they would put two lookout towers so close together. Why would they do that, Buck? Buck?"

Instantly, our lips dried and cracked, and our tongues swelled up. Jake and Lester fell on the ground, clutching their parched throats. Even though I had drunk practically a quart of water a mere hour before, I instantly became so crazed from thirst I tried to hit Buck alongside the head with a big rock. Fortunately, we had plenty of food with us, all of it dehydrated. For supper that night, we each ate a package of dry chicken noodle soup. It didn't taste too bad. As Buck said at the time, picking his teeth with a noodle, "Gloff mugghh gluddh minph!"

Early the next morning, we sprinted three thousand feet back down the mountain, tumbling over the occasional cliff in the dark, until at last Buck found a trickle of water dribbling from a crack in the rocks and forming a little puddle. In later life, I would pay as much as eight dollars for a drink in a tall frosty glass with a little umbrella and a garnish of orange slice and cherries. But never have I had a drink at any price that half measured up to the mossy, muddy water I slurped from that puddle. If I could find the puddle again, I'd bottle the water—nay, *that elixir!*—and make my fortune.

Buck's finding the water aroused in us such gratitude and adulation that we'd have built a monument to him on the spot, except we were too bruised and battered from our wild scramble down the mountain. "We will never forget this, Buck," we croaked. "You've saved us once again. Yea, Buck!"

I will mention only a few further horrors encountered

on our trek to Big Fish Lake, because I do not wish to be reminded of them more than necessary. Fortunately, a short time after Billy went temporarily mad, we intersected the very same trail we had started out on. We knew it was the same trail, because of the little signs the Forest Service thoughtfully had put up at intervals along its broad expanse to guide adventurers like ourselves.

"Just as I figured," Buck croaked. "I knew if we headed due north, we'd have to cut the old trail."

"Due west," Jake choked out.

"Whatever."

"Yea, Buck," we gasped.

"Now," Buck said, "let me check that map of yours again, four-eyes. Ah, yes, just as I suspected. There's only an inch or two between us and Big Fish Lake, provided we leave the trail and take a shortcut due east. What do you think of that?"

"Yea, Buck."

The Matterhorn, it turned out, was every bit as high and treacherous as it appeared in the movies. It did slow us down considerably, mostly because we had to substitute fingernails for ice axes and pitons. Halfway up the north face, Jake fell. Perhaps distracted by the raging storm, he hadn't driven his fingernails far enough into the granite. Even to this day I can still hear his long, shrill, warbling scream as it diminished into the dark silences of cold and empty space.

"I wish you wouldn't scream like that," I told him. "It gets on my nerves, particularly with all this cold and empty space down below."

Obviously embarrassed, Jake became defensive. "So how was I to know it was only a two-foot drop?"

At long last we found ourselves camped on Big Fish

Lake, but too tired to try a single cast. The only thing I remember about that night is that just before I drifted off, I noticed that Lester's hair had turned white. Maybe it was from the strain of our journey, or perhaps even the deep shame he felt for suggesting earlier that day that if we didn't find Big Fish Lake soon we might have to eat Billy.

The next morning we discovered that any fly whatsoever flicked out on the lake would instantly be gobbled up by a fish. It was some of the fastest fishing I've ever experienced. We also discovered that the lake had been misnamed. The fish certainly weren't what anyone would call huge or big, or even average—or even small, for that matter. I personally ate twenty-seven of them for breakfast that morning and scarcely took the edge off my appetite.

When the time came for us to head off down the trail toward home, Buck shouted, "Follow me, men! I'm going to lead you down a new shortcut I've figured out! Hup two three four, hup two. . . ."

He glanced in my direction. "And what do you think you're doing, four-eyes?"

"Don't mind me, Buck," I said. "I'm just getting out of the way."

The Two Masked Raiders

ONE HALLOWEEN A few years ago I was watching the TV news in a hotel room in a large American city. The newscaster reported that all the restaurants on the top floors of skyscrapers in the city had been sold out, because the diners enjoyed watching the flames spouting up from buildings that had been set afire by Halloween pranksters. I suppose it was something like watching a Fourth of July fireworks display, with the diners clapping their hands and exclaiming, "Oooooh! Look at that one! I liked that one best!" There were several TV shots of buildings that had just been ignited, and I studied them with considerable interest, hoping not to recognize my own hotel. Later I learned that the immolated buildings were empty, at least as far as anyone knew, but one can't be too careful in large cities nowadays.

Wanton destruction as a form of entertainment seemed

to me a bit excessive, and I was about to indulge myself in a fit of righteous indignation, when suddenly I recalled the Two Masked Raiders, who terrified our little farming community every Halloween during several years of my early youth.

The identity of the two Masked Raiders has remained secret all this time, but, under the assumption that the statute of limitations has run out on those Halloween pranks, I will now for the first time reveal the raiders' true identities: a smart, bossy kid named Vern and his sidekick, a handsome lad who bore a striking resemblance to myself.

Although the Two Masked Raiders operated over a period of only a few Halloweens, they left an indelible mark on the hearts and minds of their neighbors. Even now, when I visit the place of my youth, old-timers will mention the Two Masked Raiders to me.

"You probably don't recall, Pat, but every Halloween for years and years the Two Musked Raiders would hit our homes. It was horrible."

"*Masked* Raiders," I corrected.

"Their calling card said 'Musked.' "

"I suspect their penmanship wasn't all that good."

"If you say so. And nobody ever found out their true identities."

"Nope. Never did," I said. "They must have been terribly clever, those Two Masked Raiders."

"If you say so, Pat."

Riding home on the school bus several days before Halloween, or "Hell Night," as our neighbors referred to it, Vern and I selected our targets. "Look over there," Vern whispered. "We can hit the Millfords' house by going over their back fence, crawling across their garden, and making a dash across that open area to the chicken house. Then we can strike from behind their woodpile and be gone before they know what's happened."

"Or we could walk up their driveway," I said.

"No, no, you idiot, we can't just walk up their driveway! You don't launch an attack like that. It isn't right. You have to sneak."

"Okay."

A full week before Halloween, fear began to tighten its grip on the neighbors. We could sense it. We knew that every farmer along the highway was asking himself the question: "Will I once again fall victim to an attack by the Two Masked Raiders?" The answer was: Yes! The Two Masked Raiders spared not the old, the poor or even the infirm, although quite often they spared the really fast and mean.

By the time Halloween finally arrived, the neighbors were wild with terror, but there was nothing they could do but wait helplessly for the onslaught that would come quickly and silently out of the dark of night. Still, they tried not to show the fear that gnawed at their very innards. They went about their routine chores of milking the cows and slopping the hogs, just as if they expected life after Halloween. But this outward show of serenity did not fool the Two Masked Raiders one bit. We could hardly contain our glee over the wave of terror we had sent rolling over the land.

Occasionally, we would meet a neighbor in a store shortly before Halloween, and the subject of the Masked Raiders would come up.

"Hello, boys. I see it's about time for Halloween. I suppose the Two Masked Raiders will strike again. You boys got any idea who they might be?"

"No, ma'am. Nobody knows their true identities. Could be about anybody, but we figure they're a couple of the big kids."

"You're probably right. Well, my mister would sure like to get his hands on 'em, what they did to our place last year."

"Yeah, that was pretty awful. I mean, whatever the Two Masked Raiders did, it must have been pretty awful."

"Oh, it was! If you boys find out who the Two Masked Raiders are, you tell my mister. He'll take care of them, you bet your boots."

"Yes, ma'am."

You probably can't even imagine how thrilling it was to hear someone talk to us about the Two Masked Raiders, with that person having not so much as a clue that the ten-year-old boys being addressed were none other than the Two Masked Raiders themselves.

It is time at last to reveal exactly why the Two Masked Raiders were considered such a menace. They would streak silently out of the dark and—I realize this is shocking but it must be told for its historical significance—put little squiggles of dreaded soap on a window, sometimes even two! Then they would vanish into the night, cackling fiendishly over the havoc left behind.

Our first year out, we settled for a few meaningless squiggles. The next year, when we became the Two Masked Raiders, Vern boosted me up to a high window of the Hoff-steaders' house, a window someone wasn't likely to be peering out of, and hissed at me, "Don't do just a squiggle. Write our signature!"

"You think that's such a good idea?" I whispered back.

"Yes!"

I scribbled on the window as quickly as I could and dropped to the ground. We stepped back to study the signature.

Vern sighed in exasperation. "Not 'Pat and Vern,'" you idiot! You were supposed to write the 'The Two Masked Raiders'!"

This time I boosted Vern up, and he scribbled over our names and wrote in the signature. We stepped back to admire it.

"You wrote 'The Two *Musked* Raiders,'" I pointed out.

"Yeah, my penmanship ain't that good."

One Halloween was especially eventful. We had heard that there was a long and honorable tradition of tipping over outhouses as a Halloween prank, but indoor plumbing had made a serious encroachment in our part of the county, until only one outhouse remained, the Crankshafts'. Vern and I decided we had better take advantage of this opportunity while it still existed. Mr. Crankshaft was a huge logger, and we knew that he would have no trouble righting his privy all by himself. We crept up to the outhouse and gave it a big shove. It scarcely moved. We put our shoulders against the weathered boards and managed to rock the shack back and forth a little, but not enough to topple it. The privy was a lot heavier than it looked.

"I know what," Vern said. "What we need is a pry pole and a block of wood. We can slip the pry pole under the floor and pry it over. Do you see a pole anywhere?"

"There's one over by the barn," the privy said, in a deep gruff voice not unlike that of Mr. Crankshaft. "If you're the Two Masked Raiders, give me a minute, and I'll help you find the pole. Just stop rocking the dang privy."

The Two Masked Raiders vanished into the night.

A short while later, they were crawling on their bellies through a clover field, approaching the Rambo house. The clover wasn't tall enough to give them much cover, maybe an inch or two higher than their shoulder blades. Just as they got within striking distance, Nick Rambo burst out onto the front porch carrying a shotgun and a huge flashlight. His wife was peering out around him.

"Stand back, Judy," Mr. Rambo said. "I think the Two Masked Raiders are out there someplace."

"Are you going to shoot them, Nick?"

"Only if I see them."

The beam of the flashlight swept across the raiders, whose hair now stood several inches above the clover. Traitorous hair! Back and forth went the beam. The raiders heard the ugly sound of a shell being jacked into the chamber of the shotgun.

"What makes you think the Two Masked Raiders are out there, Nick?" Mrs. Rambo asked in a shrill, nervous voice.

"I can smell them," he said.

That was a distinct possibility and one I won't elaborate on, except to say that Nick Rambo was famous for his keen sense of smell. After shining the beam back and forth over our treacherous hair a few dozen times, Mr. Rambo and his wife went back in the house.

"I'm getting too old for these raids," Vern muttered, as we shuffled off toward home.

"Me too," I said. Nick Rambo had just aged me ten years. Even worse, though: We suspected folks of actually growing *fond* of the Two Masked Raiders! Made us pretty darn mad, too.

Mosquito Bay

MY FOUR DAUGHTERS stopped by the other day, trailed by a riotous band of my grandchildren. I make a practice to count the kids when they arrive for a visit and again when they leave, just to make sure none has been left behind. It's a simple precaution one learns after a few years of grandparenthood. When one starts to settle down in the evening with one's newspaper, one likes to avoid the shock of finding a stray grandkid hiding under it.

"Hi, Grampa!" the kids chorused, coming in and throwing their coats on the floor.

"Hi, guys," I said, doing my impression of a jolly old elf. "Ho ho ho! I was hoping you would come over, because we can play a game."

"Oh, wow! What is it?"

"It's called 'Don't Touch Any of Grampa's Stuff.' Doesn't that sound like fun? Here's how it's played. The first guy I catch touching Grampa's stuff is Out. Now, what does 'Out' mean? Your cousin Bernard could explain that better than I, although—"

"But, Grampa, we don't have a cousin Bernard!"

"Not anymore. You see, I walked into my den, and there was Bernard swatting flies with my split-bamboo fly rod, and—"

"How come you didn't want him swatting flies?"

"A very good question, Daniel. You see, it wasn't the flies I was concerned about, which is one of the reasons for my inventing the game 'Don't Touch Any of Grampa's Stuff.' So what happened, Bernard tried to—"

"Enough about Bernard!" shouted my wife, Bun. "There was never a Bernard, kids. No Bernard."

"I thought there was," I said.

"Nope, no Bernard. Now, kids, you mustn't believe everything your grampa tells you. He has a tendency to rearrange reality."

After Bun left the room, I asked the kids if they understood what Grandma meant by the phrase "rearrange reality."

"No," they said.

"Good," I said. "So Bernard told me he didn't know he wasn't supposed to play with my three-piece fly rod, and I told him that no he wasn't, because it was supposed to be only a two-piece fly rod. Then Bernard opened my big tackle box, and something came out and ate him. Does everyone understand what is meant by the phrase 'ate him'? It means Bernard was Out."

During dinner my daughters got to reminiscing and laughing about some of the wonderful times we had when they were young girls.

"Do you remember the camping trip at Mosquito Bay?" Bun asked them.

"Do we remember Mosquito Bay!" the girls shouted. "Do we ever!"

I wasn't at all surprised that they remembered that particular camping trip, because it was one of our more exciting adventures together, quite wonderful really, what you might call the perfect camping trip. Mosquito Bay is now an asphalted, fireplaced, restroomed, and garbage-Dumpstered campground, but back then it consisted only of a sliver of sandy beach embraced by dense forest. It could be reached only by boat or through the mountains by what the Forest Service maps depicted as a dotted line. Actually, the dotted line wasn't all that bad, and I managed to pilot our big old station wagon over it without any major difficulty, largely because I had grown up driving on dotted lines and had managed to develop the necessary skills. . . .

"Oh, that road into Mosquito Bay!" exclaimed my daughter Kelly. "I wouldn't have been so scared if Dad hadn't been so frenzied. When he ripped off the muffler on those rocks, that was the first time I ever knew there were so many bad words."

Clearly, Kelly was remembering some other road on some other camping trip with someone else's father. Muffler indeed! Anyway, we unloaded the station wagon, and I quickly and efficiently erected our interior-frame umbrella tent, one of those with the weird contraption known as the "spider," and rightly so. As soon as the tent was . . .

"Yeah," said Peggy. "That's the time Dad got tangled up inside the tent and screamed out, 'Help! The spider's got me by the throat!' And we all thought he meant a real spider and took off running for our lives!"

The girls all found this recollection highly amusing, I less so. As I say, I quickly erected the tent, but when I emerged, everyone had vanished, except for Bun, who was standing behind a tree with a club in hand. Once we had collected the girls from the surrounding forests, I built a fire and cooked a hearty supper, after which . . .

"Oh, I remember the fire Dad built that night," Peggy said. "We could have cooked supper just over the matches he used up trying to get it started. Then he poured his 'secret fire starter' on it. Whew! What a fire!"

"I remember that!" cried Shannon. "Wasn't he smoking at the time?"

"Yeah, he was," said Peggy. "We thought for a moment he was going to burst into flames, but he just smoked."

I myself vaguely recall that it was a rather large fire, a bit inconvenient for cooking, but nevertheless adequate for me to prepare a five-course meal.

"I was pretty little at the time," Erin said. "But I can still see him trying to cook eight wieners on the end of a long branch. It looked like he was using a spear to fight a fire-breathing dragon."

"We did have a four-course meal that night anyway," Shannon contributed. "Charred wieners, greasy buns, cold pork 'n beans, and ash of marshmallow."

Five-course meal. I count pork 'n beans as two courses, as does any serious camp chef. After this sumptuous feast, we turned in, and just in time too, because soon we began to hear the patter of rain on the tent roof. There are few sounds I enjoy more than the patter of rain on taut canvas. Now that I think of it, I really should write a book on the rearing of children in the Great Outdoors. Early on in parenthood, I noticed that my children had a tendency to pay entirely too much attention to any minor detail that caused them the slightest discomfort and as a result they missed out on the enjoyment of the situation as a whole. At the Mosquito Bay camp, for instance, they began to complain about a trifle bit of dampness in the tent, and I explained to them that they should learn to ignore such details. After which, I told them a pleasant little bedtime story until they drifted off to sleep.

"Was it the first night the bear came and scared the bejeebers out of Dad?"

"No, that was the next night. The first night an awful storm came up and blew down the tent, because Dad didn't have the tent poles connected to the spider the right way. The water was running through the collapsed tent like a river, and we were floating about on our air mattresses. What was it that Dad said?"

"Oh, it was his favorite saying in those days, whenever we complained about some awful catastrophe: 'Details! Details! Now shut up and go to sleep!' "

I believe it was on the second night of the camping trip that I detected the distinct sounds of a bear rummaging about outside the tent. I immediately got up and went outside to shoo the bear away, only to discover that the bear was approximately the size of a Buick. It was, in fact, the largest bear I had ever seen. I stood there for a minute or so, calmly studying the magnificent creature. Then, speaking firmly, to show I meant business, but not so loud as to startle him, I ordered the bear out of camp.

"It was Mom who first heard the bear," Kelly recalled. "I heard her tell Dad it was a bear."

"That's right," Shannon said. "And Dad said, 'It's just a chipmunk. Go back to sleep.' Then Mom said, 'That chipmunk just ripped the lid off the camp cooler.' "

"And Dad said, 'Okay, okay, I'll go outside and run him off.' So he lifts the door flap and looks out and jumps about three feet in the air. 'Quick!' he yells. 'Everybody into the station wagon!' "

"I thought I ordered the bear out of camp," I said.

"No," Bun said. "You ordered us into the station wagon."

"Maybe then I ordered the bear out of camp, after everybody was safe."

"No, then you got into the station wagon, too."

"Who ordered the bear out of camp?"

"Nobody. I think he spent the night in our tent, eating potato chips and reading comic books."

"Well, there you go," I said. "It is not a good idea to share a tent with a bear that is eating potato chips and reading comic books."

From the psychological standpoint, I find it interesting how the imaginations of young children, and even of a wife who at the time was scarcely out of her twenties, could distort the simple events of a camping trip so as to be beyond recognition. Even more striking, they retain these distortions into adulthood, or, in Bun's case, into grandmotherhood, and seem to regard them as factual. The horrors they reported were so far from the truth that I had no choice but to put them to the test. Surely, the girls would not wish to encounter such terrors and hardships ever again, if they had experienced them in the first place.

"For the sake of the children," I said, "whose big ears have been absorbing your fanciful tale, I offer this test. I am planning a camping trip into the headwaters of Blizzard Creek, which can be reached only by driving thirty miles on a dotted line. Who would like to go with me?"

Instantly, four daughters raised their hands.

"Very good," I said. "Now whose version of the Mosquito Bay camping trip is true?"

"Yours?" they said in unison.

"Right."

After the daughters and grandchildren had piled into their cars and headed down the driveway, I couldn't help but chuckle. I may be getting old, but my memory is still pretty darn accurate, and it would be just as accurate after the trip into the headwaters of Blizzard Creek. Opening a closet, I started rummaging around for a map and . . .

"Hi, Grampa."

Okay, so I don't count as well as I used to.

My Hike with,
ahem,
the President

WHEN RETCH SWEENEY and I came in from perch fishing one day a couple of years ago, we noticed my wife, Bun, hopping up and down on the porch. "Guess what!" she shouted. "You've been invited on a hike with President Bush!"

"You want these perch?" I asked Retch.

"No way, man," he said. "You keep 'em."

"You've been invited on a hike with President Bush!" Bun screamed.

We tied up the boat and started walking up to the house. "You lazy bum," I said to Retch. "You just don't want to spend the night fileting a mess of perch. No doubt you'll show up for breakfast tomorrow to help eat them, though."

"You guessed it," he said.

"Don't you understand what I'm telling you?" Bun screeched. "You've been invited on a hike with the president!"

"See you at breakfast," Retch said, glancing at the hopping Bun. "Might be a good idea to lock up all the sharp objects in the house tonight." He got in his car and drove off.

Bun grabbed me by my shirtfront and shook me. "Will you listen to what I'm saying! You've been invited—"

"I heard, I heard," I said. "So what's the joke?"

"No joke! You've been invited on a hike with the president. It says so right here in this letter from the White House."

I reacted to this bit of news with my usual calm demeanor, despite the distraction of Bun's repeatedly knocking me over with a feather. "When's the hike?" I asked.

"You have to leave tomorrow morning for Bakersfield."

"I'm hiking with the president through Bakersfield?"

"No, dummy, you're hiking through Sequoia National Forest, but you first have to get to Bakersfield, where you'll be driven up to rendezvous with the president."

"But why me?" I asked.

"Who knows. It's probably a mistake of some kind, but you had better take advantage of it. Not everybody gets invited on a hike with the president."

Mistake my eye. Slowly, I began to perceive the logic of it all. George Bush is an outdoorsman. I'm an outdoorsman. It made sense.

On my way to the airport the next morning, I stopped by Bob's Chevron station, the major social center in our little town.

"Been doing any fishing?" Bob asked me.

"I'm going on a hike with the president of the United States," I said.

"Oh, I've been out a few times," Bob said. "Caught some dandies off Indian Point."

"I'll be hiking with George Bush," I said.

Russell came in from the garage wiping the grease off his hands with a rag. "Hey, that's interesting!" he said.

"Yes," I said.

"Yeah," Russell said. "I was fishing off Indian Point last night and didn't get so much as a bite. What were you using, Bob?"

I tried to tell Ernie Beckman about my hike with the president, but he sped off on his motorcycle before I could get to him.

On my flight to Bakersfield, I casually mentioned to the flight attendant that I was on my way to hike with the president of the United States. "That's nice," she said. "Would you care for the Knot of Chicken or the Minuscule of Beef?"

It began to dawn on me that I didn't project the image of someone who would be hiking with the president of the United States of America. I panicked. Maybe it *was* all a mistake. Or worse yet, maybe it wasn't a mistake! Maybe I was expected to guide the president through Sequoia National Forest! It was entirely possible that the Secret Service's background check on me had overlooked the fact that I have no sense of direction and can't step ten feet into the woods without getting lost. Sure, it's a special talent, but perhaps not one the president would fully appreciate. I imagined a scene that chilled my bonemarrow: The president and I are walking down a trail.

"Look, Mr. President, huckleberries!" I point out.

"I love huckleberries," the president says. "Gosh, it's been years since I've picked huckleberries. Let's get some."

The Secret Service agents grunt sounds of alarm.

"Oh, for heaven sakes," the president tells them. "Pat

can guide me over to the huckleberries. They're only ten feet off the trail."

As midnight approaches, President Bush, two Secret Service agents, and I are probing our way through the darkened forest. An owl hoots above us. A large animal crashes off through the brush. "So, maybe moss doesn't always grow on the north side of trees," I say. "Anybody got another suggestion?"

Much to my disappointment, I discovered at the hotel that I wasn't to have President Bush all to myself. Four other writers had been invited along on the special hike, but they were all real journalists. Among them was my friend Michael Hodgson. Michael is even more adept at getting lost in the woods than I. It occurred to me that maybe presidential candidate Bill Clinton had something to do with putting the little group together. Between Michael and me, we might get the president so lost he would never be found. Talk about dirty politics!

Early the next morning we were driven to Sequoia National Forest and directed down a trail on which had been set up a magnetometer, one of those devices to detect metal you have to walk through at airports. Just as at airports, there was a table alongside the magnetometer, where Secret Service agents examined any bags or parcels. Bun had bought me a little belt pack for carrying my camera and film. The pack, unfortunately, had three zippers, one concealed. The agent could feel the film inside the pack but couldn't figure out how to get to it. He became increasingly exasperated with it and me.

"And you're protecting the president?" I laughed, only to discover that Secret Service agents have absolutely no sense of humor. (Actually, it wasn't until I got home that I said that, because I'd already discovered Secret Service agents have no sense of humor.)

The delay at the magnetometer was sufficient for me to get lost. A herd of the White House Press Corps had just thundered down the trail into the woods, and I followed aimlessly along behind, not wishing to get too close, for fear that I might get trampled or gored. Pretty soon I was lost. I hadn't realized that my little group had been led off on a different trail to meet the president for the special hike. As I was performing the Modified Stationary Panic—my standard practice in such situations—an aide to the president found me, and we raced up and down several hills until I was once again united with my group. I explained that by deliberately getting lost I was merely trying to lend a bit of authenticity to the outing, which otherwise seemed to have acquired an aura of artificiality, as hikes go, possibly because there was a Secret Service agent behind every tree. Some of the trees *were* Secret Service agents.

At last the president arrived. I was a bit surprised to see that he looked exactly as he does on TV, only a good deal more relaxed and happier. We five writers had our pictures taken with him, which was why most of us were there in the first place, if the truth be known. Obviously, the president of the United States was not about to reveal any major new policies to a little bunch of environmental writers and me out in the middle of the woods, no matter how impressive the woods.

It soon became apparent that the president hadn't invited me along as a guide, which was something of a relief. He struck off on his own at a brisk pace, seemingly unaware of steep grades, on which I thought it best to pause from time to time to check on the Secret Service agents and make sure they were all attentive. Satisfied that they were doing their work properly, I moseyed on up the hill, checking for any wildlife that might pose a threat.

Speaking of wildlife, I was beginning to think that all of it, including insects, had been removed from the park in preparation for the presidential hike. I never saw so much as an ant or a mosquito all morning. At one point, however, I was pleased to see a pair of ruffled grouse roar off from directly behind the president. He didn't seem to notice but the Secret Service agents all reached under their jackets, even as they jumped about a foot in the air. I almost burst out laughing, but restrained myself. As I say, the Secret Service agents have no sense of humor.

Eventually, the president slowed up and sat down on a log. We writers gathered around and had a nice chat with him for about thirty minutes. Several of the real journalists asked serious environmental questions, which the president casually swatted down as if they were annoying flies. I myself feel strongly that the environment is definitely worthwhile, but endless harping about it does get tedious. So I decided to ask the president a dumb question about his hunting and fishing. George Bush the outdoorsman suddenly surfaced, and he started talking enthusiastically about a fishing trip the day before: "As a matter of fact—I know this will interest you—I caught a keeper of a striped bass out in the ocean. Guys who have fished there all their lives, two of them, told me they never heard of that before, right where we go anyway. Thirty-seven inches long! I let her go, because we're trying to build that fishery back."

I've listened to thousands of such fish stories. "What!" I exclaimed. "Thirty-seven inches long! No way! You trying to kid me, George?" (I didn't really say that. I just put it in to see if my editor is paying attention.)

George Bush would make one heck of a fishing partner, I can tell you that, probably as good or better than my buddy Retch Sweeney. George would stay and help you filet the perch, too, he's that kind of guy. I was hoping we might spend a little more time together, and he would get to know me and like me, and we'd start fishing for stripers together, and then he'd offer me a small ambassadorship. Just a passing thought. But it was not to be. A pack of aides and Secret Service agents suddenly whisked him away without so much as a good-bye wave or an invitation to visit him in the White House. I was left only with some brief memories of our hike through the woods, and, of course, some photos of my old hiking pal, the president, and me to show the boys back at Bob's Chevron.

As soon as I got home, I asked Bun if Bill Clinton had called to invite me on a hike with him.

"Not yet," she said.

"That's odd," I said. "Well, we'd better stay off the phone, just in case."

Ed in Camp

WE WERE DRIVING up into the mountains. It was to be my last fishing trip with the Old Man. He was ninety, perhaps more. Probably more. It was hard to tell, because the Old Man lied about his age. He lied about almost everything. Following his conversation was like tracking a ferret through dry leaves. His name was Ed.

"I'm glad you invited me along on this fishing trip," he said. "You're a good boy."

"I didn't invite you," I said. "You invited me. This fishing trip was your idea."

"It was?" he said. "I didn't know."

"Yes, Ed, it was your idea," I said. "You said that you were going to drive up into the mountains and fish Caribou Creek one last time. As you'll recall, I told you that you couldn't drive, because you don't have a driver's license anymore. You don't have a driver's license, because you can't see more than twenty feet ahead of you. Besides, your car won't run."

"How come my car won't run?"

"Because I fixed it so it wouldn't. You may recall that you nearly ran over Mike Murphy's dog on your last outing."

"Murphy's dog should have gotten out of my way. If a dog's too stupid to get out of the way, he should be run over."

"He was tied up to Murphy's front porch, Ed. He couldn't get out of the way."

"So that's what all the fuss was about."

"Yeah. There was also some problem with a rosebush and a pink plastic flamingo."

"I hate those plastic flamingos. I must have meant to run over it."

"Anyway, I told you that if you insisted on going up to Caribou Creek one more time, I'd take you."

"So, you did invite me. You always try to put the blame on me for your own foolishness. I'd think you'd have better sense than to drag an old man like me out on a long trip like this. I'm already tired. A trip like this could kill me. I'll tell you one thing, though. One time Pinto Jack and me . . ."

I waited. "What, Ed? What about you and Pinto Jack?" No reply. Ed had gone to sleep, head back against the seat, mouth open and emitting frail little snores. Everything about Ed was frail, even his snores.

I began to wonder if this fishing trip wasn't a bad mistake. I had known from the beginning it was a mistake, but not that it was a bad mistake. Ed had already caught thousands of fish in his lifetime, many of them legal. What purpose was served by his catching a few more? It wasn't as though he had been deprived of his share of fun. He had devoted his entire life to having a good time. I doubt that a

single day had ever slipped by without Ed grabbing it in a
bear hug and squeezing out a maximum measure of enjoyment. Almost all his life, he'd been happy. I guess that's why
I hung out with him as much as I did. Maybe I wanted to find
out Ed's secret.

"Ain't you even interested?" Ed said suddenly.

"In what?"

"Well gol-dang it, ain't you heard a word I said? I was
tellin' you about what me and Pinto Jack did one time, but I
can see you ain't interested, so I guess I won't."

"Fine."

"So Pinto and me we fixed up this old school bus as kind
of a camper. Had one of them emergency doors in the back
that the kids can escape out of if they's smart enough and
want to skip school. We built a couple bunks in the bus, and
even had a trapper stove in there, with the chimney elbowed
out one of the windows. It was a real nice outfit. One week we
was camped up in McCormack Meadows, that high country
up in the headwaters of McCormack Crick, you know. About
noon one day, I fixed myself a nice baloney-and-onion sandwich and left it on the table while I went down to the crick to
get some water and . . ."

"And what, Ed?" I glanced over. He was sound asleep
again. That was all right with me. The road was getting steep
and treacherous now. The more treacherous the road, the
better the fishing, that's my theory. I punched the truck into
four-wheel drive and we started to climb. Before long, we
came to the bad spot, a big steep slab of rock that slants out
over the canyon. Even four-by-fours have a tendency to slide
ever so slightly toward the brink, just enough to give you that
feeling in your stomach that tells you the fishing up ahead is
going to be darn good. The tricky part is that the front of the

vehicle rears way up at the high edge of the rock, and you kind of teeter over the top lip of the slab and the hood is in your way and you can't see if you're going to land on the road or not, and this is very spooky because, if you don't land on the road, you're not going to land on anything for about a half mile, and all you can do then is watch the scenery flash vertically pass the windows. I've had grown men scream going over the top of the slab, and sometimes I've joined in myself, just to keep them company, and when we hit the road on the other side we'd just turn the screams into a song: *"yeeeeeaaaaaaoooooooooo,* the Old Gray Mare, she ain't what she used to be, ain't what she used to be . . ." Kind of like that. You don't want any distractions as you totter over the top edge of that slab.

"And so I start foolin' around down there by the crick, catchin' some hellgrammites for bait and . . . Dang it, stop singing about the Old Gray Mare when I'm tryin' to tell you a story. Oh, we must of just topped the slab. I didn't catch the scream part. Did we miss the road or has it just got real smooth?"

"No, we hit the road. I stopped the car to let my heart start up again. Go on with your story."

"Where was I? Hard to tell a story with you interrupting every few minutes. Oh, yeah, so I get back to the bus and my sandwich is gone. I figure Pinto snuck in and et it. When Pinto shows up, he claims he don't know nothing about any sandwich. We get to lookin' around and finally we see the damp print of a bear's paw on the linoleum. Did I tell you about the linoleum? Me and Pinto got it for practically nothin' down at the furniture store and . . ."

"Forget the linoleum. Tell me about the bear."

"What bear? Oh, yeah, the bear. We figure the bear will

come back to the bus the next day to see if we've fixed him another sandwich for his lunch. So we tie a long rope to the emergency door and hide in the brush. Sure enough, along about noon here comes the little bear, a yearling, and he hops right up into the bus. Pinto and I jerk the rope and slam the door shut." At this point, Ed burst into a long wheezing cackle. "So we got ourselves a bear trapped right there in our bus." Ed smiled radiantly at the distant memory of the bear trapped in the bus, a smile directed inward rather than outward.

"I've got a question for you, Ed," I said. "Just why did you trap that bear in the bus?"

"Why? Because it was fun, that's why. And because I reckon nobody else in the entire history of the world ever trapped a bear in a bus. What do you think of that?"

"I think you're probably right. What did you do with the bear now that you had him trapped in your bus?"

"Well, we was young bucks, so we didn't waste our time thinkin' ahead. If an idea come to us to do somethin', we did it, and left the thinkin' for after. The problem was, when we opened the door, the bear wouldn't leave. He just sat in there eaten up our grub, like he was at his own birthday party. I guess he figured it was his bus now, and he didn't seem to mind us standin' on the outside lookin' in. He seemed to think that was the way it should be. I says to Pinto, 'Pinto, we better get him out of there before he figures out how to drive the dang bus, and we'll be left stranded up here in the mountains with nothin' to eat.' Pinto says he's gettin' madder and madder just watchin' that bear eat up all our grub, and what was the bear doin' in our bus anyway, and he says he's goin' in the bus and throwin' the hairy bugger out. And he done just that. You remember, don't you, how Pinto was never quite all there? Well, by the time he got that bear out of the bus, there was a whole lot less of him there. But he done it, and that's what counts. We had a lot of good laughs over that bear, Pinto and me. Which reminds me of the time . . ."

I was staring out the windshield thinking of Pinto and the bear, and wondering whether there had been a bear, or even a bus, when I heard the Old Man's wheezing snore. Easing up on the brake, I let the truck crawl ahead until the road widened out enough for a snake to pass us on the outside edge, if he took it easy and kept himself pretty straight. Ed didn't wake up again until after we had pulled into the campsite at Caribou Creek.

I tossed the tent bundle out on the ground and started to unwrap it. Ed opened the door of the truck and looked out. "Here, stop that! You don't know nothin' about how to pitch a tent proper. Let me give you a hand with it, so it gets done right."

I spread out the ground cloth, rolled the tent out on it, and staked down the corners. "I'm almost out of the truck," Ed said. "You're stakin' them corners down too loose. Wait till I get over there and show you how."

I fitted the frame together, snapped the tent to it, and tied off the roof flaps. Then I got the two cots out of the truck and set them up in the tent, along with the camp table and chairs. I was sitting at the table pouring a cup of coffee when Ed arrived. "You should have waited for me to help," he snapped. "As usual, you done it all wrong." He sagged into a chair. "Now, I'm all pooped out from rushing over here so fast. And I left my cigars in the truck! I better go get them."

"Try to be back before dark," I said. "I don't want to have to come looking for you."

"On second thought, you go get my cigars."

"I'll get your cigars after I finish my coffee," I said. "You know they're bad for your health, don't you?"

"What health? I haven't had any health in years. Now go get them cigars, and I'll finish that cup of coffee for you. It's the least I can do."

That night I built a big campfire and the Old Man and I sat in our chairs poking at the fire with sticks, drank a little whiskey, smoked his cigars, and told stories. Ed's stories were better than mine, but only because he is such a good liar. He's also had a lot more fun. It made me a little sad, listening to all his great adventures and thinking about all the time I'd frittered away on work.

Ed leaned back in his chair and squinted up at the sky. "My," he said, "look at them stars. You can't see stars in the city. You have to be up in the mountains to really see stars. You know, there are trillions and trillions of stars. Every person on earth could have a billion stars of his own and there would still be plenty left over."

"I expect that's right," I said. "I've never thought of it that way."

"They're really beautiful tonight aren't they, the stars?" he said, gazing up into the darkness.

"They truly are," I said. "I don't think I've ever seen the stars more beautiful." Actually, I couldn't see any stars at all, because the sky was clouded over. It felt good to lie to the Old Man. I was glad to see I wasn't out of practice.

After a bit, Ed said, "You know, out here in the mountains like this, sitting around a campfire next to a fine trout stream, under a sky full of stars, why this would be a perfect time and place for me to die."

"I don't think so," I said. "It's an inconvenient time and place."

"How come? You could bury me right over there under those birches and no one would know."

"Bury you? I wouldn't bury you. Too much work. I came here to fish, not bury some ornery old cuss. You die, your remains stay right where they drop. The only trouble I'd go to is lifting that gold pocketwatch of yours."

"Robbing the dead, that's just what I'd expect of you," the Old Man growled. "You're not a safe person to die around."

I didn't much care for the morbid thought Ed was turning over in his mind. And I particularly didn't like his little musing smile. A shiver ran through me, even though the night was warm. But what does a man in his nineties have to look forward to? Right.

We sat there in silence for a long while poking at the fire. After a while, I said, "Oprah has a good show coming on next week."

"Oprah does? What?"

"Uh, pretty women who, uh, let's see what was that now? Oh yeah, pretty women who have been captured by UFO's and, uh, marry creatures from outer space and later divorce, but then have a hard time collecting alimony."

"Sounds interesting," Ed said, perking up. "I like that Oprah. She's a pretty woman. I do love them pretty women. When's Oprah have that show on?"

"Toward the end of the week. We'll be back in plenty of time."

"Good. I wouldn't want to miss it."

"I wouldn't want you to," I said.

How I Got This Way, Part II

NOBODY EVER SETS out to be a writer of short humor pieces. No little kid in the history of the world has ever said he wanted to be a writer of short humor pieces when he grew up. I was no different as a child. What I wanted to be was an artist. I drew and painted thousands of pictures from the time I was six years old until I went off to college.

"Look what I just drew," I'd say to my mother.

"Very nice," she would say. "That's one of the nicest pelicans I've ever seen." Mom encouraged me to be an artist, because she thought I was probably too dumb to do anything else. Artists don't have to be smart. All they have to be able to do is draw.

"But it's an airplane," I'd explain. "A Messerschmitt!"

"Oh, of course. I should have looked closer. I did wonder why you would draw a swastika on the side of a pelican. Just keep practicing your drawing."

Because I was planning on becoming an artist, I never paid any attention to grammar and spelling all the way from first grade through high school. Artists don't need to know grammar and spelling.

The Korean War started while I was in high school, and enlistments and the draft quickly opened up many jobs in construction. The summer I was seventeen, I lied about my age and quickly landed a job building a hydroelectric dam on a river near my home, although not all by myself. I became a highscaler, a person who hangs from a rope and pries loose rock off sheer cliffs. It was a lot of fun and I made a great deal of money. Then one day a fellow highscaler had most of the mountain fall on him. "I lied about my age," I told the foreman. "I'm only seventeen." He found me a safer job, but it involved actual work and wasn't any fun at all. After three summers of working construction, I had more than enough money to start college. Even though I was an Idaho resident, I enrolled at Washington State College, because I'd heard it had an outstanding art department. I wasn't at all worried about doing well in art, because I'd already spent a dozen years drawing and painting thousands of pictures. What worried me was Freshman English Composition. During our orientation, the college president gave a stern speech to all of us freshmen. "Look at the person on your right," he ordered. I looked at the guy to my right, but he was looking the other way. "Now, look at the person on your left." I looked at the person on my left, but he, too, was looking the other way. "Keep this in mind," said the president. "At graduation time, neither of those people you just looked at will be there to receive a diploma." Of course I felt sorry for those two guys and was happy that neither one of them had been looking at me. I still had a major worry: how to get through

English Comp. If you didn't pass English Comp with at least a *D,* you got booted out of college. The professors back then didn't want to turn loose on the world a Bachelor of Arts who didn't know how to write a grammatical and properly spelled sentence. They were worse than priests when it came to being spoilsports.

Right away, I got into trouble with the art department faculty. One day a professor asked us to name our favorite modern artist. I said mine was Norman Rockwell. I had studied his *Saturday Evening Post* covers for years. Obviously, he was on the cutting edge of modern art. The professor went into a severe fit of retching. I supposed it was because of something he'd eaten for lunch. It wasn't. He simply couldn't stomach Norman Rockwell. The whole art department faculty despised Norman Rockwell. Word quickly spread among them that Rockwell was my favorite artist, and my reputation as a serious student of art went down the drain. Also, I was having some problems in drawing class. "Why did you put a swastika on the side of that pelican?" my drawing instructor demanded.

I was faring even worse in English Comp. Every week we had to write and turn in an essay. I went through agony writing my first essay and thought that it turned out pretty well, even though I realized it probably wouldn't receive much more than a *B.* It was, after all, my first effort at serious writing. The essay came back with a large red *F* blazing on the top of it. I was shocked. And shaken. The sheer force of my anxiety impelled me to spend twice as much time on my second essay, nearly a half hour, and much to my dismay, it too came back with an *F.* It was also scribbled all over with tiny red handwriting from the professor. Three more essays, three more *F*'s. I didn't know what to do. As a last resort, I started reading the tiny red handwriting on my returned essays. It gave me some clues as to where I was going wrong, which seemed to be just about everywhere. Frantically, I started studying grammar and spelling and sentence structure. Soon I was working on English Comp essays eight hours a day, seven days a week. A major breakthrough: one of my papers came back with a *D*–. Thusly encouraged, I multiplied my efforts. I gave up dating, I gave up sleeping, and finally I even gave up Ping-Pong, of which I was dorm champion. My essay grades continued to improve. I got a *C* at last, then a *C*+, a *B*–, a *B*, an *A*–, and finally, on my very last essay, an *A*+! Ironically, that last essay was a critique and appreciation of the cover art of Norman Rockwell. "That was a great essay," my professor told me. "I was delighted to see that you decided to write about something other than chickens." That comment surprised me. After all, I had been writing about what I knew, the advice given to all beginning writers. My professor apparently harbored some prejudice against chickens, about which he had failed to inform me. What came as an even greater surprise than the *A*+, the professor recommended me for Honors English the next semester. Not bad, *F* to Honors in one semester. Mom said she had never expected any less.

By now I had invested so much time in writing essays that I decided I might as well keep on going and become a writer. The way I figured it, I could sit in a little cabin in the mountains of Idaho, write books and stories, mail them off to publishers, and they would mail me back big checks, and soon I'd become rich and famous. I didn't know why more people hadn't hit upon this very same idea. Writing books and stories was a perfect way to earn a living.

Then I took my first creative writing class. Most of the

other students, I soon noticed, seemed to be getting *A*'s for their stories, while I never seemed able to get higher than a *B*. It was discouraging. After all, if you can't be the best writer in a crummy college creative writing class, how could you ever expect to become the best writer in the world? Perhaps one problem was that I was trying to write stories that would sell to pulp Westerns, while the other students were writing about Death, Despair, and Delusion—the Three D's of serious creative writing. Before we had completed the first month of the class, at least a hundred fictional human beings had been wiped out by poverty, the crushing weight of society, or hideous disease. Suicide was a big favorite, too. Most of my characters, on the other hand, got killed in gunfights, and, by golly, they all had it coming to them. Oddly enough, the professor teaching the class—an internationally acclaimed scholar—had worked his way through college writing for pulps. I thought he should be more appreciative of my work, but he wasn't. He seemed to begrudge me even *B*'s. I decided there was nothing to do but start writing about Death, and I started pounding out a story about a woman who knocked off her husband in a rather intriguing way. A peculiar thing happened in the process. The story wouldn't go where I wanted it to go. It wanted to write itself, and at last I gave up and let it do so. Alas, it turned out not to be a serious story. I dreaded having to read it in class and, as was a requirement, explain the creative process I'd gone through in bringing this piece of, uh, literature into being. It was also the practice in that class for one's fellow writers to rip to shreds on principle anything written by anyone else, and they were seldom satisfied until the writer had been reduced to a quivering column of jelly. I began to read. From the back of the room came a snort of derision. A girl giggled. Someone tried to choke back an actual laugh. Suddenly, the whole class burst into howling mirth! It was exhilarating. I glanced up at the professor. He was bent over the lectern, wheezing with laughter! He removed his spectacles to wipe away the tears. I knew now that I could not help but extract an *A* from my creative writing professor. The story came back from him adorned with yet another *B*.

Furious, I stalked into his office. "How could you even think of giving this story a *B?*" I demanded. "I had the whole class practically rolling on the floor. You yourself laughed so hard you had tears streaming down your face."

"Yes, McManus, that was quite a funny story. But this is a class in the writing of serious literature. And even you will have to admit that your story is not serious literature."

So what could I say? Nothing! I had nevertheless learned an important lesson: The writing of humorous short stories and essays would never be regarded as pursuit of serious literature. I vowed never again to write another piece of humor. There was no future in it. Depressed as I was about that little story, I nevertheless submitted it to the campus literary magazine, and in due time it came out in the magazine, my first published work of fiction.

Writing began to dominate my life, much to the detriment of my other classes, particularly those in math and the sciences. One day I received a note from the dean of the college. He wanted me to stop by his office. I knew what it was about. Some of my grades were dismal. The dean, in contrast to myself, was a Rhodes scholar. He was not the kind of person to tolerate bad grades for long, and I knew he was about to issue an ultimatum to me. When I stopped by his office to hear the grim news, he looked up and actually smiled at me. "Ah, McManus," he said cheerfully. "Come in and have a seat. Coffee? Coke? No? Well, I just wanted to tell you personally how much I enjoyed your story in the campus magazine. I nearly laughed my head off. You, my boy, have a wonderful talent for humor. Much less so for math and science, I might add, but you are a very funny writer. Keep up the good work!"

I was of course relieved and flattered, but I wasn't fooled. The writing of humor would bring only humiliation, closely followed by poverty.

During my sophomore year, shortly after I had learned to spell *sophomore,* I got a job "stringing" for a newspaper, the editor of which always seemed to have time to sit down over coffee with me and critique my stories. He taught me just how difficult journalism is, and how extraordinarily hard it is to nail down a simple fact. Much of journalism nowadays consists of quoting "sources," which is much easier than getting down to the bedrock of fact. You can spill coffee on a newspaper today without much danger of wetting a fact, although you will drown a lot of quotes. Journalism is still a great and glorious profession, and I would not have minded at all pursuing it for a lifetime, but it is impossible to be a reporter and still live in a little cabin in the mountains.

After college I worked for a newspaper, a university, a television news department, and finally became a teacher at a university. Each job took me farther away from that cabin in the mountains. So for the first ten years after college, I worked furiously at freelance writing. I wrote articles on cancer research, arson investigation techniques, archaeology, bacteriology (one of my *D*'s in college), forestry research, wildlife research, geology (another *D* in college), art and artists, psychology, philosophy, and, oh, I nearly forgot, chickens. But never once did I think about writing humor.

My writing schedule consisted of writing every evening from seven until nine, seven days a week, every week, every month, and I sent to market everything I wrote, no matter how bad I thought something was. (Reviewer: "I suspected as much!") One day in the first hour of my writing time, I completed an article on the uses of telemetry in the study of wildlife, that is, the hooking-up of wild creatures with radio transmitters so that they can be spied upon electronically. I still had another hour of my writing time left. Well, I said to myself, I will just write nonsense for the next hour, and I did. I wrote nonsense about hooking-up wildlife with radio transmitters—all wildlife. The point was that this would do away with a lot of the problems connected with hunting. The hunter would merely have to stop by the control center and ask if a deer was in the area. The controller would say, "Yes, I see 5789-A headed for the Haverstead's meadow. At his present rate of travel, he should reach there at exactly five-fourteen." So the hunter would saunter over to the Haverstead's meadow and wait for Old 5789-A to show up. As with most nonsense, the story didn't seem to amount to much, but because I had written it, I felt compelled to mail it to market. I did, and it was rejected, no great surprise. I sent it out again, and it was rejected, still no great surprise. I sent it out again, this time to *Field & Stream* magazine. Back came a check for $300! The most I had ever been paid for an article up to that time was $750, but that particular article had taken me more than a month to research and write. I made a quick calculation. I had just earned $300 in an hour. I wrote two hours a night. Therefore, I could write two pieces of nonsense a night. That was $600 dollars a night, $4,200 a week, $218,400 a year. Why, that was more money than I could make at the university—in a lifetime! Suddenly, I became a writer of short humorous essays. A dozen or so rejections later, I sold another humor piece and then another and another. That summer I got bumped from my summer teaching job by a professor with more seniority. For the first time in my life, and that of my family, I would have to support all of us for three months solely on my writing. The family greeted this news with wide-eyed stares and trembling lips. All that lay between them and starvation was Dad's typewriter.

The day after I learned I wouldn't be teaching summer school, I went out to my sister-in-law's lake home, sat down on her dock, and pounded out two humor pieces on my Smith Corona portable. I folded up both stories, stuck them in the same envelope, and mailed them off to *Field & Stream*. Back came a check for $750, more than I would have made teaching summer school. I stood there by the mailbox, the check clutched in my hand, and stared off into space. Yes, I could almost see it out there in the distant mists, a little cabin tucked away in the mountains of Idaho.

One of the stories I wrote on the dock that day was about my miserable old dog Strange. Finally, a quarter of a century after his death, Strange, for the very first time ever, came when I called him.

And that is pretty much how I got this way.